HIGH
SCHOOL
HAZiNG

HIGH SCHOOL

HAZiNG

When Rites Become Wrongs

HANK NUWER

FRANKLIN WATTS
A Division of Grolier Publishing
New York▪London▪Hong Kong▪Sydney
Danbury, Connecticut

For
Alice Cerniglia
and
Barbara Youngblood

Photographs ©: Alfred University: 110; AllSport USA: 68 (Otto Greule); AP/Wide World Photos: 48 (Bill Haber); Archive Photos: 16 left (HO/Reuters), 16 right (Joe Traver/Reuters); Corbis-Bettmann: 21, 29 (UPI); Courtesy of Gettysburg College Library, Courtesy of Hank Nuwer: 18 (Broken Pledges, 1990); Courtesy of Alice and Dale Haben: 83; Courtesy of C.H.U.C.K.: 67; Courtesy of Hank Nuwer: 53 (Photo Courtesy of A. Hueton, Broken Pledges, 1990), 11 (Photo Courtesy of Edd Lockwood, Broken Pledges, 1990), 10; Courtesy of Hank Nuwer and Maisie Ballou: 112; Courtesy Rita Saucier: 115; Liaison Agency, Inc.: 47, 99 (Douglas Burrows), 102 (Deborah Copaken), 43 (Renato Rotolo), 39 (Paula A. Scully); Omni-Photo Communications: 59 (B. Richmond Smith); Photofest: 32, 69, 94, 95; Robert Landau: 25.

Visit Franklin Watts on the Internet at:
http://publishing.grolier.com

Library of Congress Cataloging-in-Publication Data

Nuwer, Hank.
    High school hazing : when rites become wrongs / Hank Nuwer.
      p.   cm.
    Includes bibliographical references (p.) and index.
    ISBN 0-531-11682-4 (lib. bdg.)   0-531-16465-9 (pbk.)
    1. High school students—United States—Conduct of life. 2. Hazing—United States. 3. Initiations (into trades, societies, etc.) I. Title
LA229.N893 2000
373.18—dc21   99-33768
                                                     CIP

GROLIER
PUBLISHING

"The individual embodies a moral strength that groups and organizations do not possess."

—Reinhold Niebuhr

CONTENTS

INTRODUCTION

As a lifelong "joiner," I always felt that hazing was something I could not avoid. At age eleven, after joining the Boy Scouts, I was made to clean summer camp latrines and was constantly harassed by some older scouts. Later, in high school in western New York, some students asked me if I wanted to join their underground fraternity, which I was eager to do until I learned that the price of admission was a vicious paddling. I declined. However, in college, lonely and eager to socialize with women from sororities, I joined a fraternity and did whatever the senior members demanded. At Buffalo State College, I was forced to run long distances, perform calisthenics, submit to mild paddling, eat raw eggs, and endure other bits of foolishness.

Nor did I escape hazing in the workplace. One summer in college I worked in a

Author Hank Nuwer (in checked jacket, third from left in second row) belonged to a Buffalo State fraternity where he was hazed as a pledge.

plant that supplied coking coal to the steel industry. Older workmen put new fellows such as me through stupid, onerous, and painful tasks. About a dozen other college students quit after one day on the job.

At all levels, the hazing I endured stopped once the senior members decreed I was one of them. After I was initiated into a fraternity, I continued the tradition, putting the new "pledges" through some of the same stunts I myself had hated. It was not until I attended graduate school at the University of Nevada, Reno, that I saw the real danger and cruelty of hazing.

Some acquaintances of mine in a college club held a drinking spree for acceptance into the group, even though the university had suspended all club activities for previous violations. One giant young college football player, John

Davies, participated in the spree, ultimately paying a horrible price: he died of alcohol poisoning. John left behind a grief-stricken family, his friends—who had been unaware how deadly alcohol can be—and a sadder, wiser campus community. John's family tried to get the legal justice and civil court systems to punish the club, but no individuals were found legally to blame for John's death.

That awful event occurred in 1975. I have written about hazing ever since.

I wrote about John's death for a national magazine in 1978. Ten years later I received a Gannett Foundation grant to study the problem of college hazing. My research helped me write two books about fraternity and sorority

The Sundowners at the University of Nevada, Reno, used to pour alcohol into the mouths of their pledges during initiations. Pledge John Davies died of alcohol poisoning in a club initiation in 1975.

initiations—*Broken Pledges* and *Wrongs of Passage.* I also interviewed former soldiers and marines, including drill instructors, for a magazine story on military hazing that was published in 1999.

As I see it, part of my job as a journalist is to help keep track of hazing incidents in the United States. As a result of my books, articles, and television and newspaper interviews, high school students and parents often contact me about new incidents of hazing. I have spoken with many young people traumatized from hazing, as well as their parents, high school coaches, school board members, and administrators. I have also interviewed hazers.

This book looks at actual hazing incidents that have occurred mostly in the last ten years in U.S. high schools and other institutions. The stories you are about to read are not pleasant—by being informed, however, you will be far less likely to go along with the crowd. You will read here, for example, the stories of young lacrosse club members at Western Illinois University who initiated a rookie athlete who died a few hours later. They told me their troubling, deeply personal stories as part of their sentence for serving alcohol to a minor.

In this book, I have tried neither to overestimate nor underestimate hazing dangers. While I condemn the practice of hazing, which has led to many deaths in college, endangered the lives of high school students, and thrown the hazers and hazed unwillingly into the public spotlight, I take a "hate the sin and love the sinner" approach.

High School Hazing is a guide to help the hazed say no to these practices as well as a reference book. But it is also for hazers, for the practice of hazing cannot end until older students realize what they are doing and step forward courageously to help younger boys and girls. Making a decision to say no to hazing and stand up to a group takes a lot of courage and reasoning. Too many high school students allow the pressures put upon them by their peers to cloud their judgment and make them say yes when they mean no.

If you think you know about potentially dangerous hazing practices, tell your parents, a teacher, your principal, or a police officer right away before anyone is hurt. You may have to talk to two or three adults before you find someone who can help and understands. Unfortunately, too many coaches and educators continue to dismiss initiation activities as harmless or even beneficial for building unity. The more educators and researchers learn about hazing, the less chance there is that the practice will continue unchecked. If you and your parents, teachers, or coaches would like to write me about experiences with hazing, send an E-mail message to nuwer@ibm.net.

Hazing has existed for more than two thousand years. Must we wait another two thousand years for it to end? Hazing activities won't end on their own. Stopping them takes swift, strong action by committed young individuals, with the assistance and guidance of responsible adults.

I hope this book takes the magic out of hazing and exposes it for the cowardly and brutal practice it is. Once you understand why students haze and submit to hazing, you'll not only be able to resist getting involved yourself, but you'll be able to talk sense with your classmates before they make mistakes that could haunt their lives forever.

—Hank Nuwer

Chapter One

A MATTER OF DEFINITION AND HISTORY

Hazing isn't a one-size-fits-all social problem. Some male and female students, particularly those who rarely get involved in school activities, go through secondary school without ever facing an initiation. Hazing may also be uncommon at schools where an enlightened administration has forbidden the practice and enforced stiff penalties for hazers.

However, at less vigilant high schools, people who tend to get involved in clubs and activities may be subjected to hazing not just once but many times. A few go through one outrageous initiation after another and may in turn subject others to similar treatment.

Hazing can start a few days or weeks after students begin high school. If freshmen join sports teams or the cheerleading or pom-pom squad, they may find themselves subjected to abuses that older classmates tell them everyone before them has endured. And should they decide to join a gang or high school secret society, new students will likely find themselves facing the roughest initiation rituals of all.

Hazing does not always stop after graduation from high school. Anyone following current events has seen that military hazing is getting more violent and dangerous. A number of videotaped initiation ceremonies on the evening news has shown a practice known as blood pinning in which senior paratroopers slam the sharp points of ceremonial wings savagely into their charges' bare chests.

College initiations—particularly in fraternities and, to a lesser extent, sororities—have been more deadly. Hazing and pledging activities have caused at least fifty-six fraternity and sorority deaths from 1970 to 1999.

Alcohol-related fraternity deaths are sobering. In 1994, MIT freshman and fraternity pledge Scott Krueger (inset) died at a Boston hospital, apparently of alcohol poisoning.

AN OLD CUSTOM

Hazing is not a new phenomenon and no generation has a monopoly on foolish initiations. It existed in ancient and medieval schools in Greece, North Africa, and western Europe. For hundreds of years and into the twentieth century, fashionable secondary schools in England such as Eton had a problem called fagging. Upperclass students used younger classmates mercilessly and cruelly as glorified servants. A new student did not worry *if* he would be hazed, for that was a given, but how long it would take him to gain acceptance so he could take revenge on the next unfortunate new boy.

On the American frontier, newcomers in town—called greenhorns and other mocking terms—showed their willingness to gain acceptance by enduring a little debasement. Often they would undergo discomfort by taking a "hazing" from old-timers. The term *hazing* then referred to driving cattle. Sailors sometimes used the word to refer to water dunkings and other initiations given to first-time crossers of the equator. It also was a term used in many of the first private and public colleges in America.

In the early 1900s, many college presidents believed that a system of hazing was an acceptable way for older students to teach newcomers respect for their school or organization. If first-year students learned their place, the reasoning went, they would honor their elders. It wasn't long before a romantic myth that such ill treatment was a tradition for everyone's good took root.

Hazing in the early 1900s often didn't end well, however. In 1911, at the University of Texas, a hazing victim shot and wounded an upperclassman who was tormenting him. At Saint John's Military College in Maryland in 1914, a victim who had been hazed shot a bullet from his gun through the door of hazer William R. Bowlus and killed him. And at the University of South Carolina in 1916, a first-year student was twice savagely bloodied in beatings—

once in an initiation and once because he reported his injuries to the school's administration.

When real incidents of hazing by older peers did occur, there were few opportunities to get satisfaction in court. The few hazing laws in existence were seldom enforced. Even when a young college male bled to death following an accident during a University of North Carolina initiation in 1912, the perpetrators were brought to court on manslaughter, not hazing charges. When found guilty in the death of freshman Isaac Rand, the students were turned over to their parents instead of being jailed.

Gruesome hazing is not a recent phenomenon. In this early photo from a Gettysburg (Pennsylvania) College fraternity, members wore hoods and blindfolded initiates as part of their hazing rituals.

HIGH SCHOOL HAZING—A GROWING PROBLEM

While high school initiations have existed in some form in the United States for much of the twentieth century, the practices were usually either too minor to be widely reported or school administrations and parents worked to keep the nasty details from being revealed. When shameful events did occur to freshmen or athletic team rookies, victims often kept their stories to themselves.

In the 1970s and 1980s, some high school students—seemingly searching for rites to mark their passage into adulthood—began to conduct initiations that resembled brutal university hazings. By 1990, hazing incidents occurred nationwide with enough frequency to alarm educators.

Today, hazing at secondary schools ranges from an insignificant issue to a rampant problem. In some schools, enforcement and scandals haven't seemed to eradicate the problem. In fact, incidents have often become more sadistic and dangerous.

As reports of hazing are heard more frequently on the nightly news, in school board meetings, and in professional journals, one conclusion is unmistakable: hazing in high schools across the country is becoming an increasingly pervasive problem that students, parents, school administrators and educators, and communities must address—and in a preventive way.

The type and range of incidents required for initiation vary greatly. In Massachusetts, some Duxbury High School baseball players wore their uniforms while pulling off a ritual-like shoplifting spree. At schools in Illinois, New Jersey, and Vermont, among other states, high school males and females have had to simulate sex. For years, actual sex has been required of girls—known as Queen Bees—who become associated with gangs. Beatings and paddlings for admission into high school organizations have taken place in Massachusetts, Missouri, New Jersey, New York, Ohio, Pennsylvania, and Texas.

Often alcohol is added to an initiation, increasing the likelihood of something going out of control as the inhibitions of participants drop and their motor skills become compromised. A Santa Fe, New Mexico, high school student nearly died in a homecoming initiation when he drank so much that his blood-alcohol level was three times the legal limit for an adult to operate a vehicle in that state. Today's high school hazing contributes to the continuation of hazing in colleges, the military, professional sports, secret adult societies, and some occupations. Hazing must be seen as a widespread problem that is not limited to but born in secondary schools.

HAZING BY DEFINITION

The first newspaper record of a high school student dying in an apparent hazing incident occurred in 1905, although there certainly may have been other cases that were recorded as accidents. William Taylor, a thirteen-year-old student, died on February 10, 1905, as a result of contracting pneumonia. "Hazing Kills Schoolboy" read the headline in the *New York Times*. Taylor was accosted by older schoolboys on his way to school and held down on the ground while snow was pushed down his clothes.[1]

Whether this death would today be deemed a result of hazing is unclear. A coroner might conceivably rule that the incident had only exacerbated an existing physical problem. And to be ruled hazing, not just boisterous behavior, it would have to be shown that the incident was a school group initiation. Today, for example, high schools and colleges often try to classify incidents as mere horseplay, because educators are either trying to protect their school's reputation or they don't truly understand what activities meet the definition of hazing.

Defining hazing precisely can be difficult. Administrators have long used the term *physical hazing* to refer to hazing that could cause bodily injury. *Mental hazing* was harassment that frightened new students into thinking they were going to be punished far worse than planned or have to carry out some taboo activity such as stealing. Sometimes mental hazing escalates into physical hazing, as when a student is forced to strip and then endure a whipping or paddling.

In general, however, hazing can be defined and identified. In all cases, hazing involves activity that requires new members to show subservience to older members of the group, lowering the self-esteem of newcomers. Not all high schools have the same definition. Dexter (Maine) Regional High School in its 1999 policy defined hazing as "any action or situation which recklessly and intentionally

Initiations are usually an exercise of power over others. These pledges had to strip and submit to paddlings. After a dousing, they were forced to mop the drenched floor.

endangers the mental or physical health of a student enrolled in a public school."

One of the more specific definitions of hazing is stated in the antihazing policies adopted by Richfield Public Schools in Minnesota. Hazing means committing an act against a student, or coercing a student into committing an act, that creates a substantial risk of harm to a person in order for the student to be initiated into or affiliated with a student organization, or for any other purpose. A student organization means "a group, club, or organization having students as its primary members or participants. It includes grade levels, classes, teams, activities, or particular school events." Even underground or unsanctioned school groups fall under this definition.

A DEFINITION OF HAZING

According to policies published by Minnesota's Richfield Public Schools, hazing includes but is not limited to:

1. Any type of physical brutality such as whipping, beating, striking, branding, electronic shocking, or placing a harmful substance on the body.

2. Any type of physical activity such as sleep deprivation, exposure to weather, confinement in a restricted area, calisthenics, or other activity that subjects the student to an unreasonable risk of harm or that adversely affects the mental or physical health or safety of the student.

3. Any activity involving the consumption of alcoholic beverage, drug, tobacco product, or any other food, liquid, or substance that subjects the student to an unreasonable risk of harm or that adversely affects the mental or physical health or safety of the student.

4. Any activity that intimidates or threatens the student with ostracism, that subjects a student to extreme mental stress, embarrassment, shame or humiliation, that adversely affects the mental health or dignity of the students or discourages the student from remaining in school.

5. Any activity that causes or requires the student to perform a task that involves violation of state or federal law or of school district policies or regulations.

FROM FOOLISH TO DANGEROUS PRACTICES

Initiations used to consist of putting on silly clothing, wearing garish makeup, sporting handmade signs, or doing errands. For example, new members of the Future Farmers of America (FFA), a national organization in many high schools where students have a farming background, sometimes have to wear a drawing of a green hand around the neck to show new-convert status. In another example, a rookie football player in New York state was taped head to foot. Increasingly, however, these stories of noncriminal hazing have been replaced by acts most observers would regard as cruel and dangerous.

At this time, unlike the most severe college hazing incidents, high school hazing is rarely deadly. However, a number of close calls lately have made educators afraid that high school initiations could evolve into deadlier forms. This has led to increased efforts to make junior high and high school students aware of potential dangers.

Hazing at the high school level sometimes involves dangerous alcohol consumption, paddlings, or savage beatings—which could easily cause permanent injury or death. Forty-one states with antihazing laws now ban these three activities as criminal hazing, though some states such as

Virginia require proof of physical injury before police officers can make an arrest. In 2000, the state of Vermont took testimony to decide whether to join the other forty-one states and pass antihazing legislation.

THE NEED TO BE ACCEPTED

What is the purpose of hazing? Remember that all groups need to induct new members or risk dying out. Hazing reassures senior members that the new people value membership in the group. Members willing to gain acceptance through hazing may be logically a little less likely to change the old organization the senior members know and love.

In fact, a new group member who refuses to accept hazing is usually (albeit unfairly) considered a deviant, according to researchers in group behavior.[2] And through the socialization process students go through in the elementary grades, they grow increasingly less likely to intervene to help someone else in a crisis situation—particularly if group members are picking on a single individual. Studies have also found this to be the case when police officers in a group can't seem to stop beating someone.[3]

Furthermore, new people who refuse to be initiated— even if they find the activity repulsive—often feel uncomfortable, seeing themselves as abnormal. It may be hard for a high school administrator or parent to understand why this is so, but people have a need to be accepted and valued by their peers. "All of us are very hungry for that sort of thing," says group psychology expert Irving L. Janis. "None of us can get enough of it."[4]

People outside a group—having no need to belong— may find it hard to understand why newcomers to a group crave acceptance from insiders to such a degree. The urge to belong is powerful. In high schools where popularity is particularly valued, there should be little surprise that nonmembers might envy the status members possess. "If I can only join this group," the newcomer thinks, "then others will envy me."

Advertisers who sell automobiles, fashionable clothing, and jewelry use this same kind of pressure to great economic advantage. "The state of being envied is what constitutes glamour," writes one expert on consumer thinking.[5]

Even adults can lose their judgment when it comes to hazing. Professional athletes, secret society members, some secret nonsanctioned police societies, and members of the military all have been involved in hazing incidents. Even U.S. Coast Guard enlistees taking their first passage by ship

Teenagers aren't the only group to crave acceptance. In this degrading initiation at a baseball fantasy camp, adult newcomers are sprayed with shaving cream and beer.

over one of the Great Lakes have endured shocking treatment at the hands of second- and third-class petty officers, sitting naked in tubs of ice water filled with refuse, accepting sexual abuse, and eating globs of shortening covered with hot sauce and tobacco juice.[6]

If adults will put up with such mistreatment for acceptance, how far will vulnerable high school students go to fit in? It's no wonder both male and female high school athletes, members of the Future Farmers of America, pom-pom squad members, cheerleaders, and so on have demonstrated their willingness to accept almost anything during initiations.

A TRADITION OF DECEIT

One reason hazing continues year after year is that members who have suffered vulgar, demeaning, and dangerous practices believe it will restore some of their own lost dignity. To do otherwise would require members to admit that the hazing they endured was pointless and wrong. It would also require them to go against their peers to protect younger students, some of whom appear eager to endure the humiliating practice for tradition's sake.

Nor can the element of revenge as an inspiration for provoking hazing be underestimated. Just as study after study finds a relation between victims of abuse later turning into abusers themselves, so too do high school authorities and college officials hear hazers explain they were only doing what had been done to them as newcomers.

Nearly all acts of hazing involve deception. Hazers lie all the time to newcomers. First they lie about the severity of the hazing, which is intended to build fear in the initiate. Then as newcomers invest more and as the initiation process nears an end, hazing escalates, always remaining secret. Hazers also lie to one another, to adults, and to themselves to rationalize that the brutal practices build group unity.

When an initiate gets hurt, hazers quickly try shifting the blame from themselves onto the victim. In particular, they try to insist that the victim was a willing participant. Many states have passed hazing statutes that say a victim's consent for some or all of the proceedings has no bearing in the prosecution of a case. Other states put more responsibility on victims, saying that the victim had to oppose the ordeal and feel stress throughout the entire initiation.

Chapter Two

RECOGNIZING HAZING

Because hazing emphasizes conformity, individuals who differ from the crowd because of their independent thinking, sexual orientation, appearance, or race seldom fare well in mass initiations. Some hazed students can even experience a kind of post-traumatic stress disorder, a condition soldiers in combat sometimes suffer from when exposed to horror, terror, or shame.

Injured students are doubly confused when administrators, teachers, coaches, and even parents appear to back the hazers as a way to build school spirit and unity. For example, after an athlete at an Allentown, Pennsylvania, high school was injured in a hazing during the early 1990s, a coach lost his temper and hit a hazer. In response, the parents and school board members focused on the coach's response instead of on the seriousness of the incident itself.

If authorities judge that an activity violates a state statute against hazing, initiations can be a criminal matter. But because law enforcement officers and prosecuting attorneys don't always understand the dangers of hazing, and

In the past, rituals such as New York University's outdoor paddlings of pajama-clad freshmen were considered harmless fun that boosted school spirit.

arresting young people can be unpopular with the public, hazing incidents that appear to be a criminal matter sometimes end up being ignored or dismissed. In Pennsylvania, Washington, and other states, statutes against hazing meant to cover college fraternity hazing have been interpreted in such a way as to rule out enforcement for high school hazings altogether.

Over the last decade, high school hazing scandals have divided communities into angry camps in Arizona, California, Hawaii, Illinois, Massachusetts, Minnesota, New Hampshire, New Jersey, Ohio, Texas, Utah, Vermont, Washington, and Wisconsin. Smaller problems with initiations have occurred in almost every other state in the Union.

The first step in putting an end to dangerous initiation practices is learning to recognize hazing in all its guises.

ATHLETIC HAZING—A COMMON NUISANCE IN HIGH SCHOOLS

Most often, high school educators are faced with athletic hazing. Here are just a few recent instances.

- In 1999, football player Matt Warnock suffered a head injury after he was jumped by McAlester (Oklahoma) High School teammates in a locker room hazing by teammates that more closely resembled a gang initiation. It was the second hazing injury involving the football team in two years. The incident angered the student's mother who demanded that the football team be shut down, just as fraternity chapters are closed when members are caught hazing.[1]

- In 1997, Westlake High School officials in California canceled the wrestling team's season after allegations that some older wrestlers probed the buttocks of younger wrestlers with a mop handle they had nicknamed Pedro. In 1999, newspapers reported that while hazing had occurred, the offenses were likely less heinous than first reported. No charges were ultimately lodged against the wrestlers, though one of the victims said he had been the target of jokes and called a homophobic term.[2]

- In 1996, a sophomore football rookie was injured during traditional hazing at the high school in the

Hempfield (Pennsylvania) Area School District. Nine veteran players admitted involvement. The incident resulted in a school statute allowing for expulsions in future hazing cases. The lack of a policy in this case undercuts assurances made by many educators and school boards that existing statutes already cover hazing.[3]

- A brutal paddling of eight freshman football players at Alexander High School in Albany, Ohio, led to a suspended jail sentence and community service for the team captain. A similarly vicious paddling of seventh-grade football players by older junior varsity veterans led to the suspension of eight boys at Chicago's St. Edward Catholic School.

FRESHMAN HAZING

Like athletic hazing, initiation of high school freshmen or eighth graders is quite common. According to research published in the *Pittsburgh Post-Gazette*, in one Pennsylvania middle school, there is a day when older students kick the new sixth graders. In the state's Mt. Lebanon school district, another school has a variation where new seventh graders are shoved roughly.

Many schools quietly permit some mild forms of embarrassment, capitulating to student desires to keep some traditions. Sometimes, it is because administrators think that they can only set limits on activities and not eliminate them entirely; other times, it is because the adults believe traditions should be upheld.

In a June 1998 incident, eighth-grade boys planning to attend Severna Park High School in Maryland in the fall were attacked at their bus stop and paddled from the legs upward by four high school eleventh graders. One of the victims reported the occurrence to police and second-degree assault charges were filed.[4]

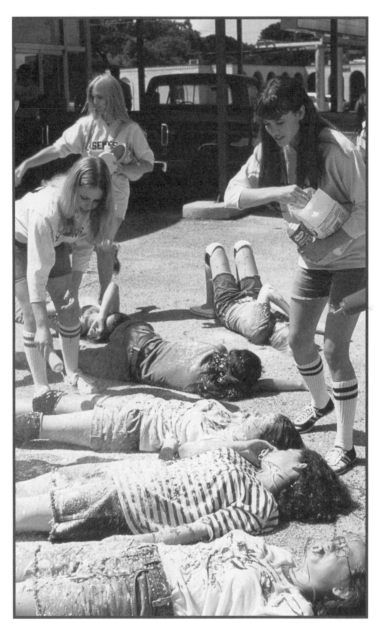

High school students initiating freshmen is common. In a popular film about hazing, *Dazed and Confused*, freshman initiations include mustard, ketchup, whipped cream, and flour.

In a 1996 incident in Arlington, Texas, a Lamar High School hazing occurred in which sixteen older students covered six sophomores with excrement, beer, and other substances and paddled them. The hazers were convicted of hazing and received a sentence of community service instead of jail. "The intent may be benign, but the consequences can be devastating," one Lamar school official said. "When you mix youthful petulance and alcohol and other substances then you've increased the risk substantially that someone could get seriously hurt."[5]

However, at California's Monta Vista High School, school officials introduced positive teamwork exercises to welcome freshmen, replacing a former tradition where older students inked the faces of new students with markers at a traditional dance.[6]

HAZING IN POM-POM AND CHEERLEADING SQUADS

Many school districts wait until a major hazing disaster occurs before implementing a formal policy. So it was with Glenbard West High School in Glen Ellyn, Illinois, which did not do so until 1993, when the *Chicago Tribune* exposed the humiliation of new Topperettes, the school's pom-pom squad.

The hazing practice involved some forty male and female students. It began by smearing new girls' faces with foodstuffs. At a private home, older cheerleaders asked the younger girls to pretend they were performing a sexual act on the male students, who had no ties to the group. The new girls agreed; some were horribly distraught. After the older Topperettes finally brought the shaken girls home at 3 A.M., some parents found out about the initiation from their daughters. School authorities and critics of hazing decried the simulated sexual acts, and passage of a strict anti-hazing policy soon followed.[7]

Another reprehensible hazing of pom-pom and cheerleading squad girls took place at Buffalo Grove High School in Illinois. Unfortunately, it is not unusual for similar or even copycat hazing practices to occur at nearby schools after an incident is widely reported in the media.

FRATERNAL GROUPS

High school fraternity hazing incidents sometimes make the newspapers but much less frequently than those in college fraternities. On the other hand, college fraternities are much more active about educating their members and introducing zero-tolerance policies toward hazing than high school fraternities are.

Many states now frown upon high schools permitting students to affiliate with national fraternities at all. The more-than-one-century-old Phi Kappa National Fraternity has been chased out of all states except Alabama and Mississippi. The reason became clear in 1999, when dozens of fraternity members from Mississippi became drunk and trashed furniture at a Phi Kappa hotel party; police arrived on the scene to arrest underage drinkers. The incident illustrated why so many educators feel that the fraternity's original purpose of good fellowship has become nothing more than an excuse for young males to party without restraint.[8]

NOT JUST IN HIGH SCHOOL

School officials often point out that hazing is common among teen groups outside of school. In one 1994 lawsuit in California, a fourteen-year-old claimed he was the victim of hazing by older boys at a church-sponsored summer camp. In a 1995 lawsuit, grieving California parents argued that their twelve-year-old son had been killed in a hazing incident when older boys caused his bicycle to swerve in front of a bus.

In 1998, while I was teaching a course at Ball State University, one of my students told me that at age fifteen he had unintentionally injured a new caddie in a traditional initiation at a golf club. In the prank, two veteran caddies would insert a broom between a victim's legs to give him a brief ride. "Nick didn't get right back up," said Mark Patterson in an essay about the incident.[9] "He looked up at me with pain written all over his face. . . . His arm was bent in places it shouldn't have been."

At first Mark and his cohort made up a story about the caddie being hurt in a basketball game, but Mark's conscience wouldn't let him rest. His boss reprimanded him in "language Andrew Dice Clay would be amazed at," said Patterson, who still works as a caddie to put himself through college. "I wanted to run away but I didn't, and I am proud of myself for that. But my days of giving the younger guys a ride they will never forget have been long over."

IS HIGH SCHOOL HAZING GETTING MORE BRUTAL?

Certain types of initiation rituals appear to be more severe than twenty years ago. After a potentially fatal 1998 lake-dousing initiation of eighth graders by Interlake High School students in Washington resulted in several expulsions, police theorized that the stepped-up hazing might be tied to the general level of violence in society. In the 1980s and 1990s, killings and violent attacks during gang initiations may also have contributed to a sense that initiations are supposed to be rough.[10]

One thing is clear: hazing has grown more brutal. Following are four areas of hazing that are particularly troublesome.

- Some older athletes have become more willing to commit acts of same-sex rape against rookies with or without the knowledge of the coach. In Texas in the mid-1990s, a high school coach's contract was taken away after school board members heard evidence that football rookies had coat hangers inserted into their rectum by veterans, and that the tradition had been in place for perhaps five or more years (see Chapter Four for more about athletic hazing).

- A few high school social groups and upperclassmen in some high schools have been requiring teenagers as young as fourteen to consume potentially lethal amounts of alcohol to join their ranks (see Chapter Five for more about hazing and alcohol).

- The ritual of savage beatings is required by street gangs and even juvenile clubs in small towns such as Flanagan, Illinois (see Chapter Six for more about gang initiations). Even more reprehensible, gang initiations in Texas, Illinois, Wisconsin, Arizona, and other states sometimes order members to have sex with young girls, often by rape. Victims as young as ten or eleven are made to roll dice to see how many males will participate in the assault.

- The involvement of high school females in cheerleader, pom-pom, sorority, and freshman class hazing is on the rise and may have unfortunate implications for national college sororities. Up to now, although some violent hazing, alcohol misuse, and even branding have occurred in college sororities, hazing has been far less a problem in female clubs than in male fraternities.

Already, however, high school hazing by girls may be having an influence on younger children. Administrators at Lincoln Middle School in Hawthorne, New Jersey, suspended seven eighth-grade sorority members for paddling an initiate in 1996 until her buttocks were severely bruised. The inspiration for the action may have been hazing activities of Hawthorne's high school students, which have long posed problems for administrators.[11]

EDUCATORS UNEDUCATED ABOUT HAZING

Educators used to tout the concept that education was a privilege and that initiating newcomers, within reasonable bounds, was a symbolic paying of dues. In other words, new students were expected to show deference to older, wiser classmates. Old notions die hard, and a few educators today still spout the same tired philosophy that should have died out long ago.

Here are some examples.

- After a hazing incident said to have involved indecent assault and battery in a western Massachusetts high school football camp, the superintendent reduced penalties for hazers to a three-day suspension, saying, "Boys will be boys."[12]

- "We have to be careful, as educators, that we allow the kids to have their fun," said South Fayette School District (Pennsylvania) superintendent Linda Hippert. Hippert maintains that rituals establishing tradition are proper if supervised by adults. High school juniors in the district do acts of servitude for seniors on a certain day. No doubt these youngsters will wonder what is wrong with doing the same in college. But if these activities were carried out by fraternity pledges in Pennsylvania, it could result in the fraternity receiving a brief suspension of privileges at all colleges in the state.[13]

- In Texas, during the 1990s, anyone who failed to report a hazing incident could have faced criminal prosecution. But, in 1999, the law received legal challenges from those who said it deprived an individiaul of the right to remain silent if accused of a crime.

What is needed is a way to make school officials realize that they don't get to decide whether or not an initiation constitutes a crime; local police and prosecutors do. In Wisconsin, for example, the principal of Deerfield High School did not consider a 1998 initiation—in which a freshman baseball player was taped to a bench and nearly urinated on by a veteran player whose pants were already unzipped—"a police matter," so she didn't report it to authorities.[14]

BEFORE THE 1990s

In the 1970s, schools for the most part ignored initiations that stayed within certain boundaries or disciplined offenders quietly without much newspaper coverage. In contrast, newspaper coverage of college fraternity hazing was extensive between 1970 and 1979, when twenty-three males and two women perished as a result of reckless initiation and pledging activities nationwide. Between 1960 and 1969, there were two deaths in college student clubs, a substantially smaller figure, but one that should have been taken more seriously as a predictor of hazing behavior to come.

Alcohol was a major factor in many of the 1970s hazing deaths. An upsurge in drinking during initiations contributed to a big leap in fraternity-related fatalities. There also were at least seven fatalities during student club parties from 1970 to 1979 because of alcohol poisoning, falls, and auto accidents. And one Sigma Nu member from the University of North Dakota, terrified that he was going to get a "pink belly," a painful stomach bruising often given as punishment to football players, stabbed a fraternity brother to death in 1979.

Hazing in the 1980s caused problems in certain pockets of the country, including high schools from California to Massachusetts, as well as in some initiations in the workplace. For example, in the late 1980s, an eighteen-year-old female ambulance trainee died after chugging a fifth of

Alcohol and forced drinking continues to be a major factor in hazing deaths.

whiskey at her initiation party. The volunteer fire department—a group that should have known about the dangers of alcohol better than anyone—dumped her into her car to let her sleep it off. The victim's mother sued the crew and won a judgment of $380,000.[15]

In Texas, senior girls at Barbers High School in Chambers County reportedly initiated students by covering them with a mixture of manure, syrup, and rotten eggs. Some parents threatened to harm physically any senior caught hazing their children. Others retorted that the tradition had been around for four decades and that no one had ever complained until "Yankees" had moved to the area from the North.[16]

And in California, a boy injured in a fight following a hazing incident sued the Corning Union High School District for a deviated septum he said he suffered as a result of the school's failure to supervise students. A court awarded the boy a small settlement to cover some medical expenses.

HORSEPLAY AND HAZING

Traditionally, harassment on school grounds that does not involve an initiation is usually considered horseplay, not hazing. In a number of cases of horseplay, school administrators and police have considered bringing hazing charges against a juvenile. For example, when a tall fourteen-year-old football player from Scituate High School dropped a tiny fourteen-year-old student on his face, causing severe damage to his teeth and gums, the school's principal told a reporter that the Massachusetts hazing law might cover the incident.

In such instances, however, because the case does not meet the state statute definition of hazing and is likely to be thrown out of court, leveling charges of hazing may be counterproductive. Horseplay injuries probably are best handled by prosecutors as an assault-and-battery offense.

School administrators have to educate themselves more precisely about what behavior is considered hazing and what is not. In particular, all coaches, administrators, and teachers need to be familiar with their state statute on hazing and keep up-to-date with amendments to the law.

For now, some schools assume that all students who take part in an initiation or team ritual must be doing so willingly—an assumption that antihazing activists strongly denounce. After Pennsylvania's Keystone Oaks High School football players shaved their heads (the way the Indiana Pacers basketball team and other pro teams have done), a school spokesman insisted "they did it willingly . . . as a unity thing."[17] An antihazing activist would argue that because of the dynamics of hazing, victims cannot truly give consent and are therefore forced into participating in initiation rites.

In states without hazing laws, the public sometimes fails even to hear of hazing incidents in high schools. In Denver, Colorado, a 1997 *Rocky Mountain News* editorial complained that the Aurora police department, at the insistence of the county's district attorney's office, had clamped down on releasing details of what was called "violent hazing" at Overland High School. In the end, however, the newspaper did report the incident—a freshman hazing beating in which older students covered a new student's head with a pillowcase, then throttled him.[18]

Chapter Three

RISKY BEHAVIOR

The April 1999 massacre at Colorado's Columbine High School of twelve students and one teacher by two teenagers whom their peers described as outcasts has drawn long-overdue public attention to the everyday pressures and violence in U.S. high schools. This chapter looks at teen behavior in relation to hazing and peer-targeted initiation abuse.

In spite of the recent media coverage of high school hazing, the topic has been largely insufficiently studied. However, at last some insight into the effect of bullying, hazing, and harassment on high school students might be found. A study on those activities, funded by the U.S. Justice Department, began in 1999. It is being conducted at North Thurston School District in the state of Washington. The school, selected at

In the aftermath of the Littleton, Colorado, massacre, the public and the media have re-examined high school life and rites.

random, suffered a football team hazing not long before the grant money was awarded.[1]

THE NEED TO SEE HAZERS AS THEY ARE

Because many participants in nongang high school hazing are regarded as "good kids"—sports captains or class officers, with passing grades and generally polite school demeanors—a principal, coach, or school board will often downplay bad behavior in initiations. This tendency of superiors to want to see good in those they are predisposed to like is called the halo effect. It is a tendency that people in charge have to guard against.

Some educators say that people who are hazed consent to hazing and can say no at any time. These educators fail to see that, when it comes to hazing, consent is meaningless.

Victims give it without getting full disclosure from hazers and without really knowing what the initiations will involve. Hazings are unpredictable. Not even the hazers can say exactly how the initiation rituals will turn out. That's why when someone is hurt, a hazer is sure to respond that no one ever meant for *that* to happen.

Only when hazing turns out to involve paddling, sexual assault, or criminal activity do such authority figures typically reverse their earlier favorable judgments of the leaders orchestrating the initiations. Put another way, the halo effect too often allows angels in appearance only to get away with deviltry.

BAD DECISIONS

Peer pressure is usually a major factor when otherwise responsible, intelligent teenagers make bad decisions. Nancy Adler, a California health psychologist, notes that peer pressure is important when sexually active teenagers decide, for example, whether or not to wear condoms. "The immediate experience is what matters to them, not worries about long-term consequences," said Adler, in a comment that just as easily pertains to hazing.[2]

One problem is that until teenagers mature, they may have a skewed sense of reality. "By age ten or so, they enter a risky period when they do lots of exploring at a time when their cognitive development has not yet reached the point where they can make judgments that will keep them out of trouble," says New York child psychologist Beatrix A. Hamburg. "They cannot really comprehend laws of probability. And they also have ideas of invulnerability that persuade them that they can safely take a known risk."[3] Even worse, immature teenagers who survive some sort of risky behavior or get away with a bad decision think their odds of doing so in the future are as good or better, not worse.[4]

And of course, the ability of teenagers to make good decisions only worsens when they are under the influence of alcohol, making hazing practices even more dangerous. It is hardly surprising; many studies point to alcohol use in high school as a leading cause of truancy and problem behavior.

POST-HAZING EMOTIONS

Just as peer pressure is put on freshmen to go along with hazing, so too is there pressure put on victims after an initiation, as hazers and their friends cajole, threaten, and shun the victims. Like rape victims, victims of hazing sometimes fail to press charges or mysteriously rescind them days later. In 1998, three young male high school wrestlers in southern California who allegedly had been initiated by veterans suddenly asked, through their parents, that the investigation be halted.[5]

In addition to the shame hazing victims may feel after being touched inappropriately during an initiation or being forced to do something they consider wrong, hazers often avoid the initiates. Studies on the effects of guilt show that people who feel they have wronged another person tend to avoid that person's company.[6]

Victims often feel a loss of esteem and trust when they realize the true character of the older students they have admired. Worse, while the victim feels isolated, the hazers may continue to be idolized by other classmates. Until these classmates mature, they will tend to give an unusual amount of respect to peers who are good at sports and reject those peers who have well-developed moral qualities but may lack athletic skills.[7]

A LOSS OF COLLECTIVE SENSE

Why do people seem to lose their collective sense during initiations? Evidence exists that people tend to act more recklessly in the presence of others than alone.

Researchers at Columbia University found that the presence of others in a potentially life-threatening situation causes individuals to display less-than-usual caution, not more. Researchers learned that students in a potentially dangerous situation are less likely to seek assistance if other people are around than if they are alone.[8]

FOLLOW THE LEADER

The emotional and physical gap between a high school freshman and high school senior is wide. Socially, the two differ in sophistication, dependence on parents, and ease of relationships with the opposite sex. Erik H. Erikson, author of *Identity: Youth and Crisis*, notes how the end of childhood is marked by "new identifications" with peers and leader figures.[9]

Primitive societies and many religions anticipated the need for rituals, which served to prevent what Erikson terms "role confusion." The rituals, among other things, marked the end of a childhood and the beginning of adulthood.

Young people in today's world do not have an abundance of formal rituals to celebrate growing up. Instead, there is emphasis on the concept of reaching a legal age to gain privileges. At various ages, young people look forward to the right to drive and the right to vote. Some anticipate reaching twenty-one to drink liquor legally in the United States.

With rites of passage in short supply, today's youths have turned to cliques for their rituals. Cliques include gangs, fraternities, sororities, sports teams, and other "insider" groups. Many have their own lingo, jokes, mannerisms, preferred style of dress, way to wear makeup, car preferences, and tattoos. Some revolve around illicit drug use, alcohol abuse, and criminal or outlaw activities.

Group leaders and individualists may depart from the norm in their selection of clothing or hairstyle, but chances are their choices will be consistent with hot new fads from MTV or the latest movie attracting a teenage audience. And it's not just teenagers looking for new styles—advertising firms and clothing and athletic shoe manufacturers go

Members of a Hispanic gang from Los Angeles flash their group's sign.

boom or bust depending on how well they set or follow trends.

Members have common interests and dislikes, including professional sports teams, music groups, hangouts, and hairstyles. They have similar attitudes toward drugs, cigarettes, and alcohol. Users tend to regard the nonexperimenter as the deviant, while most adults hold the opposite view.

Clique members, believing themselves rugged individualists, ironically lock themselves in the most rigid conformity. They tend to look at themselves through the eyes of peers to judge themselves "winners" or "losers." Imitation of high-status peers is frequent. Members may even use a similar gait when they walk together.

Some teenagers may spurn contacts with adults other than the ones they see in institutional settings such as church and school. They may choose adult role models who project antisocial, rebellious images such as gang leaders, rock stars, and "bad boy" athletes.

After the New Orleans Saints conducted a 1998 hazing no different from a savage gang "jump-in," or beating, the team was left with two severely injured first-year players. Rookie Cam Cleeland was sidelined with an eye injury he sustained when bashed with a bag of coins. Jeff Danish was thrown through a window; he was hospitalized for stitches. The National Football League set a horrendous example for high school players by allowing these hazers to play during the 1998 season.

Hazing also occurs at the professional level. After his eye was injured during a training camp hazing incident, New Orleans Saint Cam Cleeland (right) sits out a 1998 practice.

TWO TYPES OF HAZING

Hazing often takes two forms. One method is for veterans to use harsh treatments, shunning, and ridicule to cause prospective members to quit. The other is to put desirable prospective members through ordeals and stunts to test them, accepting them fully afterward.

The second type of hazing has several intentions. There is the aim of getting younger members to break ties with parents, transfer loyalty to the team, and show willingness to do anything for the group. Veteran members may also try to break down the newcomer to fit the organization's personality.

Sometimes the aim is to make overachievers feel like misfits, getting them to do less well academically to bring them down to the level of the rest of the group. Exceptions may be made for top athletes, musicians, or actors who are perceived by their peers as having a chance "to make it" someday.

All of these hazing activities force the newcomer to display conformity. Those who are hazed lose power; those who haze regain lost power by exercising authority over others.

BREAKING THE PARENTAL TIES THROUGH ABDUCTION AND SECRECY

Although some activities designed to force newcomers to yield power once seemed to exist solely in colleges, they now occur occasionally in U.S. high schools, such as the practice of abducting, or kidnapping, recruits.

In 1995, the practice of kidnapping at Reed City High School in Michigan was stopped at least temporarily when the father of an abducted student threatened to press charges.[10] Yet adolescents are often reluctant to confide in their parents about initiations since those very rituals are meant to celebrate their own progress toward adulthood and a breaking of parental ties.

Fears of getting caught by authorities sometimes make hazers conduct initiations secretly in remote places, a condition that can lead to deaths or serious injuries with no hospitals close by for help. Sinclair Skinner, an African-American high school student from Tampa, Florida, explained in a 1999 interview that the biggest concern of members who hazed during his initiation into a high school service club was being caught by the police.

Skinner's initiation began with an uncomfortable interview as members asked him if he had ever had sexual relations or if he was a drinker. "We then had to be blindfolded and taken to rough neighborhoods in the city in pairs while in our underwear. If you [two] were the last to make it back you would not be allowed in the organization. The last trial was an obstacle course called 'the trail' where you ran through this thick underbrush in your underwear while the members hit you and threw eggs and tomatoes. The service clubs had rivalries based on who had the toughest initiation." Skinner, now an activist-member of an African-American college fraternity, wants to see an end to brutal hazing practices.

"PRETTY SICK" TRADITIONS

An overenthusiastic or reckless group of individuals can increase the severity of the usual initiations with catastrophic consequences. For example, hazing practices during homecoming at two public high schools in Santa Fe, New Mexico, have included kidnappings, head shaving, and abandonment of bound students. Santa Fe High School directing principal Aaron Trummer told a *Santa Fe New Mexican* reporter that homecoming abductions were "a pretty sick tradition that has been on this campus for years. . . . The reality is, our kids see no purpose in homecoming so they create a purpose."[11]

Upperclassmen at many schools across the country turn freshman year into a reign of terror by hazing. In

Thousand Oaks, California, eighteen Newbury Park High School seniors smeared mustard and syrup over freshman girls and walked others—wearing dog collars—around the school on leashes in November 1994. In Buffalo Grove, Illinois, more than a dozen athletes and cheerleaders at Buffalo Grove High School were suspended in 1996 for covering younger students with cat litter, hair removal formula, and urine. In Houston, Texas, cheerleaders at Midland High School were suspended in 1996 after they isolated one girl and poured chocolate syrup all over her clothes. Also in Texas, nineteen high school students in a San Antonio suburb were suspended after pelting new cheerleaders with eggs and asking them to mimic sexual acts with male athletes.

Adolescence is a time when males and females are expressing a strong curiosity in their sexuality. It is not surprising that so many initiation horror stories in high school today include simulated sex. Once again, adult supervision and education are essential to curtail this kind of behavior.

One reason hazing is so objectionable is that it often involves crude sexual innuendo, outright touching of genitals or simulated sex, and forced or "encouraged" drinking through dares and intimidation. Rather than allowing each boy or girl to move toward adulthood at his or her own pace, it instantly plunges young people into many of the vices of adulthood.

British novelist Charles Dickens, writing in a different context—about child labor—summed up perfectly the reason that school districts should end hazing. "It always grieves me to contemplate the initiation of children into the ways of life when they are scarcely more than infants," noted Dickens. "It checks their confidence and simplicity . . . and demands that they share our sorrow before they are capable of entering into our enjoyments."[12]

WHEN HAZING TURNS INTO ABUSE— MALE ON MALE

Rosalind Miles, author of *Love, Sex, Death and the Making of the Male*, warns that males in "overtly masculine" roles show "an obsessional insistence, jokey but menacing, on phallic power and supremacy." Whether on a high school sports team or in the workplace, some males joke about anal rape or conduct initiations involving acts of anal penetration with objects. These male players make quite a show of their homophobia, and occasionally, like their coaches, taunt rookies with slang terms for women and gays, says Miles. They are simultaneously hostile toward rookies and dependent on their coaches for approval.

In high school locker rooms across America, given societal pressures not to make a scene, and the strength, size, and violent natures of these hazers, athletes horrified by vulgar hazing often keep silent. If they appear to be nonconformists, they may face the wrath of the veterans themselves.

"UNCOMFORTABLE" PRANKS

Many hazing practices are more repellent than violent. In Baker City, Oregon, three seniors in the fall of 1996 disrupted a pep rally by splashing four dozen first-year students with buckets of a foul-smelling concoction. The mixture contained canned squid, salsa, soup, and other substances, according to police. The three conducting the initiation were charged with criminal mischief and harassment. The young men said they thought the incident would be viewed as a prank and stressed that nothing in the mixture hurt anyone.[13]

This response is typical; male and female teenagers— and college fraternity members—often defend hazing as "fun." This type of humor is associated with aggression. Its

At Ontario's Lakehead University, a revolting 1983 freshman initiation required students to immerse themselves in a ditch filled with cow manure, fermented wheat, and sawdust.

purpose is to denigrate a newcomer or group of newcomers, elevating the senior members by lowering the newcomers in their own estimation and that of others.[14]

Adolescent humor is keyed into the interests and taboos of the age level. Because of parental pressure about good grooming, hygiene, appropriate dress, and proper behavior, many initiations lampoon these exact constraints. Male and female teenagers require new members to dress in inappropriate clothing or outfits that parody the clothes of an infant or a member of the opposite sex. Some initiations require students to get as filthy as they can or put shaving cream or toothpaste into newcomers' hair. At Interlake High School in the state of Washington, the scene of hazing incidents since at least the mid-1990s, freshman girls were restrained by older students and "covered with sanitary napkins," according to their statements to the *Seattle Times* in 1996.[15]

Simply put, adolescent hazing often has a strong "gross-out factor," with teenagers dreaming up initiation stunts that they would find repugnant under most conditions. Their aim is to make newcomers mildly to extremely uncomfortable. They don't count on the situation getting out of hand or on injuries when newcomers resist and resent the mistreatment.

A CLIMATE WHERE HAZING FLOURISHES

Why does hazing flourish in so many high schools? It may have something to do with the fundamental drawbacks of the U.S. educational system, which is charged with serving the needs of a great many young people.

Some social critics see inevitable clashes in high schools, where the values of thoughtful individuals—students and teachers—collide with the values, or lack of them, in a mass-market culture.

Edgar Friedenberg, author of *Coming of Age in America: Growth and Acquiescence*, believes adolescence is a rich time full of opportunity, when teenagers should celebrate their uniqueness. Instead, many high schools act as an extension of the larger "manipulative mass culture," which can blot out originality in young people. Friedenberg finds this fact shameful: "The meanest and most-cringing sycophant, the blandest and slyest bureaucrat, were closer to being human in adolescence than they were ever to become again."[16]

While students are, of course, in high school to learn literature, mathematics, science, and history, they are doing many things of greater importance. They are learning about respect for the rights and property of others, collaboration, patience and understanding, and the importance of rules—

all crucial things for civilization, writes educator Neil Postman in *The End of Education*. Moreover, students are at work developing and defining their very selves.

Unfortunately, say critics, something bad happens along the way in the American educational system. Because the mission of high schools is to educate everyone, high schools quash some individuals with strong, different self-identities. Some individuals are brilliant introverts who reject much of the teenage culture. Others claim a different sexual orientation.

Students who attack others sometimes act on cues from some teachers and administrators. Often, these adults' words and actions teach the students that nonconformists have two choices—assimilation or isolation. Thus, high school hazing of freshmen and rookies can be particularly vicious when directed toward nonconformists struggling to find an identity.

The typical American high school, charges Friedenberg, is so intent on enforcing conformity that it discriminates against any student who resists entry into the teenage culture. The result is the death of individual identity in a young person. "In a little while, it is as if he had never been," writes Friedenberg.[17]

As previously noted, this desire to enforce conformity explains why many educators in the 1800s, preferring absolute order to the flourishing of individual identities, encouraged hazing. They wanted hazing to quash the exuberance of new students and remind them of their lowly place at the bottom of the educational food chain. Today, some still publicly agree.

In Idaho, school administrators at Shoshone High School came under public fire in 1994 for criticizing a young man who refused to undergo an initiation. Initiations were important for school spirit and to create "bonding," said the school superintendent. High school coaches sometimes believe that initiations foster team discipline and confuse conformity with discipline.

THE CONSEQUENCES OF HAZING

Who are the losers when hazings occur? Everyone. The victim is traumatized, emotionally violated, and often hospitalized. Those who remain uninvolved but quiet are tortured by their own cowardice.

Hazers may be the biggest losers of all, for they have chosen the roles of brute and abuser—an identity that keeps them from taking large, important steps to break free. And, although it is frightening to consider, some athletes who haze may themselves become high school educators and coaches.

The U.S. system of secondary education is also a big loser. "The highest function of education," writes Friedenberg, "is to help people understand the meaning of their lives, and become more sensitive to the meaning of other peoples' lives and relate to them more fully." Education, he stresses, should help us all "transcend our own immediate environment."

High school hazings, in short, are an obstacle to that process. They are now institutions in which critical thinking skills get dashed, people learn to relate only to others like themselves, and students are enslaved rather than transcend their environment.

"What the public schools do now expresses their actual position in society," writes Friedenberg. "Any major change in the social function of the schools must come from a corresponding change in the relationship of the school to society. And the society, itself, is too contemptuous of human dignity . . . to tolerate such a change."[18]

The community of Columbine High School in Littleton, Colorado, and the general public learned a terrible lesson in 1999. The two teenagers who killed thirteen people, including several athletes, with assault weapons and homemade pipe bombs had themselves been socially ostracized by football players and the "in crowd." While athletes at Columbine deny that the slayers had been harassed, other witnesses said that gunmen Dylan Klebold and Eric Harris had been routinely shoved into lockers and ridiculed. What is clear is that a number of hazing victims at the college level, dating back to the early 1900s, have retaliated with deadly results out of an indefensible but genuine belief that they were defending themselves. If hate crimes and hazing are to stop, students need to learn to respect one another and their schools from the day they enter as freshmen until the day they graduate as seniors.

Chapter Four

HAZING ATHLETES

Rituals are an important part of high school and college team sports. Heated debate between students, coaches, parents, educators, school board members, the media, and even community leaders usually accompanies any attempts to change or do away with certain high school traditions.

POSITIVE RITUALS

Some traditions are essential to high school student life and are intended to provide future graduates with positive experiences, cherished memories, and rituals marking the transition into adulthood. These traditions include pep rallies, marching bands, a homecoming dance yoked to a big football game, winning a conference trophy, a statewide individual athlete honor, an annual all-star game, and spirited rivalries with other schools. In smaller communities, adult citizens even identify with their high school football or basketball teams' successes and failures, as *Hoosiers*, a film about high school basketball, demonstrated so well.

Other rituals, though less ceremonial, may have great meaning for student athletes. They include getting a uni-

Many high school rituals are positive and valuable to student body and community alike.

form, moving from the junior varsity team to varsity, receiving a varsity letter symbolizing athletic excellence, and cutting down a basketball net after a victory. In addition to the satisfaction of winning and playing one's best, these rituals contribute to making dedication to practice, sacrifices of leisure time, and lost social opportunities seem worthwhile to dedicated athletes.

To students outside the athletic arena, as well as to athletes, varsity letters and trophies are usually regarded as symbols of accomplishment to be admired. An athlete's talent can eventually result in induction into a high school or college hall of fame—or even offers of college scholarships or jobs playing as pro athletes.

NOT JUST FOR BOYS

The hazing of high school female athletes is historically more controlled than male athletic hazing. Most high school girls' athletic team incidents are handled by school boards and administrators. Here are some recent exceptions which made it into the newspapers:

- Two female Clintondale (Michigan) High School softball players in 1992 removed a freshman teammate's ponytail with a knife and threw it out a school-bus window.[1]
- A girls' soccer team initiation involved partial disrobing on the grounds of a Hawaii high school in 1997.
- In Spokane, Washington, a predawn initiation involving Mead High School female varsity soccer players took place in 1998. Stunts included players being taped to a trash can and having their hair covered with toothpaste and cheese spread.[2]

PEER PRESSURE AND TEAM UNITY

Behind the scenes in high school and college team sports, peer pressure is evident even without initiations. Individual high school athletes put pressure on themselves to win, to represent their institution, and to appear tough and unbeatable to rivals. Even teams that refuse to haze cannot ignore the presence of peer pressure. Each team's structure includes team captains, self-driven leaders, and seniors who have influence and who dominate the collective personality of a team.

Student athletes and coaches realize that to win consistently a team needs solidarity and chemistry as well as athletic talent. Getting a team to function together isn't easy with a diverse group of high school players from different economic circumstances or ethnic groups. One unfortunate way that some teams try to socialize athletes is to haze. And coaches may go along with the practices because they were once athletes in the same system.

But players and their coaches, viewing hazing as a quick way to achieve group unity, underestimate the repercussions that hazing can have on the hazed and hazers alike. The benefit of hazing is overrated and is a common misconception in high school sports.

WHY HAZING CAN HURT A TEAM INSTEAD OF UNITING IT

While a recent study says harsh initiations might inspire people to show more devotion to a group or team, the fact is that hazing creates tension and behavior that can be destructive and divisive. No one intends for initiations to go wrong, but youthful adrenaline and the occasional addition of alcohol can lead to reckless behavior. In the end, initiations often injure players physically or psychologically, especially if the hazing has violent or sexual overtones.

Coaches, athletic directors, and school administrators frequently say they had no clue hazing was going on when there is evidence to the contrary. Team initiations are often conducted in secrecy. When administrators and law enforcement officials try to investigate hazing incidents, they report stonewalling by everyone involved, including the hazed rookies themselves. When newspaper reporters phone school officials for comment, calls frequently go unreturned. School boards often put a cloak of secrecy around a scandal in an effort to keep information from the public they are supposed to keep informed.

For example, in 1981, a potentially dangerous and highly irresponsible soccer team ritual called Freshman Kill Day was uncovered at Toms River (New Jersey) High School South. Rookies each year were beaten, kicked, slammed into mud puddles, and then washed down with hoses. Though the event had gone on since 1973, neither the school board nor the parents had ever done anything to stop the "tradition." Interestingly, when the school board finally did take action by terminating the contracts of the three soccer coaches, many parents were so committed to a winning tradition that they demanded the coaches' reinstatement.[3]

WHY DON'T HAZED ROOKIES COMPLAIN?

Hazed rookies refuse to inform authorities for many reasons. Some feel intimidated or fearful. Some feel the hazing they endured has granted them a valuable status. Others shrug off the hazing because they have been through worse in other organizations. Since quitting the team or letting the leaders down are such taboos for most players, it is not surprising that rookies hide mistreatment. Complaining to the school administration might get veterans suspended, hurting the team's chances for success and ruining the whistle-blower's relationship with the team. Exile in the form of quitting the team becomes necessary to get away from the shunning that is sure to come.

TYPES OF ATHLETIC HAZING INCIDENTS

Hazing practices most commonly involve intimidation, practical jokes, forced workouts, alcohol consumption, and demeaning treatment. High school or college rookie athlete and cheerleading initiations in the United States have included all of the following behaviors, which range from the somewhat harmless to the dangerous and offensive:

1. Blindfolding rookies and making them do stunts

2. Smearing initiates' bodies with whipped cream, mayonnaise, raw eggs, and other foods

3. Ordering new cheerleaders to put on garish makeup, then ordering them to sing in front of students in the cafeteria

4. Taking new cheerleaders in pajamas to breakfast in a public place

5. Making rookies push pennies down the halls with their noses

6. Covering rookies' clothing with ink

7. Forcing male and female rookie players to drink enough alcohol to result in intoxication, vomiting, or poisoning

8. Holding a mock court with punishments meted out by a mock judge

9. Cutting, greasing, or dyeing rookies' hair

10. Shaving males' body hair or pressuring athletes to shave their heads

11. Putting an intoxicated player in a car trunk for a ride in the winter

12. Taping nude male rookies so that they are immobile and humiliated

13. Carrying out sexual abuse against rookies or forcing male or female rookies to simulate sexual acts

14. Ordering female rookie athletes and cheerleaders to perform demeaning activities in front of male outsiders and occasionally strangers in bars

15. Forcing rookie swimmers to drink alcohol and then jump into the pool

16. Making rookies purchase alcohol for veterans

17. Playing silly games to embarrass players (such as a board game played without clothing)

18. Putting a broomstick handle or other objects in a male player's anus—an activity that fits the definition of criminal sodomy in several states

19. Stuffing rookies inside equipment bags

20. Making male rookies race one another with a cookie, cracker, or olive in their buttocks' cheeks with vile consequences for losers

21. Forcing rookies to sit nude on ice blocks

22. Making rookies eat pubic hair

23. Subjecting rookie players to "butting," in which the rookie player is held down while a veteran puts his naked buttocks in the player's face

24. Beating the rookies or making one rookie wrestle several veterans or run through a gauntlet of team members hitting or paddling the rookies

25. Stripping rookies in the locker room and throwing them outdoors into the snow

26. Using objects such as severed heads of cows and chickens in a fetish-like manner

27. Making a new member carry a chicken with a string connected to his penis

28. Pouring grain alcohol down the initiate's lips and lighting a match, resulting in burn wounds

29. Making rookies carry veterans' equipment and food trays

30. Striking rookies with a rope, a belt, or a flattened hand to cause welts or cuts on their chests and stomachs

31. Giving wedgies by lifting a rookie by his underwear, sometimes by jamming a hockey stick in underwear and raising him, or hanging rookies by their jockstraps from coat hangers

32. Making rookies jump off a 10-foot (30-m)-high wall

33. Digging a pit and filling it with unpleasant substances that new players must jump in

34. Making rookies eat ultraspicy food stuff or vile concoctions of food in so-called stews

35. Dousing male rookies with perfume

36. Making rookies form a lineup and receive verbal abuse and sometimes shoves

37. Ordering rookies to run, do drills, or perform calisthenics until they drop, as punishment for real or imagined offenses

38. Applying liniment to a rookie's groin or buttocks

39. Having male baseball team rookies slide into mud puddles around bases on a diamond after a rainfall

THE ROOKIE AS A SPORTS INSTITUTION

One obstacle to getting rid of hazing among athletes is the institution of the rookie. Traditionally, rookies have been treated as untutored and unimportant members of the team who deserve the ill treatment of wily veterans.

Athletes—both rookies and veterans—derive their identities from their teams. Even if all hazing were to end tomorrow, the concept of rookie status would remain. Hazing can be a way for a veteran to face the threat of a young rookie who may in time displace and humiliate the older player. In turn, rookies may agree to hazing to show submission to the veterans and speed up the acceptance process.

HARASSING THE NEW ARRIVAL IN COMMERCIALS AND ON PRO TEAMS

In 1987, Pizza Hut earned national embarrassment after anti-hazing activists blasted a television commercial depicting a fraternity hazing and pressured the company to drop the advertisement, which Massachusetts state congressman John Bartley called "utterly tasteless." In the 1990s, one television network showed a film clip of a Cincinnati Bengals quarterback gleefully leading veterans on a mission to initiate new rookies. And the ESPN sports channel has aired a commercial promoting itself that shows veteran sports commentators staging a mock hazing of new commentators. While most news articles have taken hazing incidents seriously, that has not always been true of sports columnists and reporters, who often make light of hazing.

Today's professional athletes rarely, if ever, haze in a way that can be said to threaten the lives of rookies. Some professional basketball teams have rookies carry the equipment of veterans all preseason and sometimes all season long. Seating on planes for many National Basketball Association teams is by seniority—veterans in first class and rookies in coach class with fans. Indiana Pacers basketball rookies sing at the start of the season. St. Louis Cardinals baseball rookies dress up in female wigs and dresses.

One member of the National Hockey League Hall of Fame, Doug Harvey, who died of cirrhosis in 1990, used to terrorize rookies. According to the *Sporting News*, he once started a fire in a railroad car women's restroom to flush out a young man whom he and Montreal Canadiens teammates intended to initiate.

GROWING PUBLIC AWARENESS

The scrutiny of hazing in educational institutions first came from the outside, not inside. The public began expressing collective indignation after Chuck Stenzel died in an alcohol-related initiation for a fraternity popular among

This is Eileen Stevens's favorite photograph of her son Chuck Stenzel, who died in 1978 while pledging a hard-drinking athletic fraternity at Alfred University.

varsity football and lacrosse players at Alfred University in New York. During part of the initiation, pledges were locked in a trunk with the real or implied assumption that they had to drink the alcohol that was given to them.

The media had a handsome youth's face to attach to hazing—and Eileen Stevens, a grieving but fearless mother who verbalized what was wrong with such "isolated" incidents. In 1979, Stevens appeared as a guest on several national talk shows before millions of viewers. She announced the forming of her antihazing organization CHUCK (Committee to Halt Useless College Killings).

BARRY BONDS SPEAKS OUT AGAINST HAZING

As a student at Arizona State University, Barry Bonds declined to join a fraternity, in part because he didn't want to go through hazing and have his peers boss him around in the name of brotherhood. "That wasn't my style," he said. "I listen to my parents enough. I don't need to listen to somebody who's not my parents."

Bonds

Bonds has said he is in favor of better education programs to make students aware of the hidden dangers of hazing. "These hazing things are going on in these colleges and children are dying for it," Bonds told the *Arizona Republic* in 1994. "It needs to stop. . . . I would like to play more educational roles . . . [and] put an educational program out there and allow people to see what reality is. Not so much *Sesame Street* and things like that. That's been going on for years. But reality. The real world." In fact, in 1994, Bonds played a New York senator who fights for a tough state hazing law to prevent deaths in the made-for-television network movie *Moment of Truth:*

Actress Linda Gray (in the role of Eileen Stevens) and Bonds in a still from a network movie about hazing (for which author Hank Nuwer served as a consultant)

Broken Pledges, based on the true story of Chuck Stenzel.

In short, Bonds feels young people will always be subjected to peer pressure, but that's all it is—pressure. In the end, the individual can say yes or no. One challenge facing educators in the new century is to help students say no to hazing, drugs, and gang involvement.

SEXUAL ASSAULTS AS A PART OF ABUSE IN ATHLETIC HAZING

In a 1984 athletic hazing case, seven junior varsity players from Nogales High School in Arizona said that they had been sexually assaulted by older players in the back of the team bus. Four of the young athletes sued the Nogales

Unified District, eventually settling for $138,000. Although there were four coaches present during the incident—who were roundly criticized for neither being aware of the incident nor intervening—a jury acquitted them. After the incident, all four had their coaching duties taken away.[4]

Unfortunately, high school administrators often respond poorly to these hazing incidents. In some cases, perpetrators receive harsh punishment; in other cases, they go practically unpunished. Some teams that hazed have had to forfeit games and see their hopes for championships end when veteran players are booted off the team, and in a few cases, out of school. Other hazers merely apologize, with a punishment of one- or two-game suspensions.

A few cases have gone to trial. In 1992, some wrestlers at Johnson Creek High School in Wisconsin admitted taping a student but denied sodomizing him with a mop handle as the victim claimed; they were acquitted.[5] That same year, Bryan Brownlee, aged fifteen, charged that his anus had been penetrated with a mop handle during an attack by several Sunnyside (Washington) High School wrestlers. Dozens witnessed the attack, which caused internal injuries and later prompted the victim to seek therapy. Four wrestlers were charged with second-degree rape, but after extensive plea bargaining, the charges were reduced substantially. One eighteen-year-old wrestler, Richard Melendrez, entered a guilty plea to second-degree reckless endangerment and received a 150-day sentence with a ninety-day suspension. The rest were allowed to serve in a work-release program or were convicted of less serious offenses.[6]

DOES LIGHT PUNISHMENT ADD FURTHER INSULT TO HAZING INJURIES?

On a number of occasions, victims and their parents have complained that hazers are punished too lightly. For example, in 1985, after two Lowell (Massachusetts) High School hockey players suffered serious injuries, including broken ribs and a bruised kidney and abdominal wall, the school superintendent merely banned practices run by hockey team captains.[7] Unmollified, the parents of one victim, Michael DiGiovanni, demanded serious penalties for the hazers. The school board suspended five athletes for what was left of the hockey season.[8] In the aftermath of the suspensions, the school's hockey coach quit, denying it was from any pressure to resign. Nonetheless, the incident was just the tip of the hazing iceberg for Massachusetts educators.

Coverage of hazing in Massachusetts exploded after Mary Lenaghan—mother of an American International College student killed in a 1984 initiation for a fraternity of athletes—revealed that widescale, long-term athletic hazing was present at her son's high school. Football rookies at Watertown High School had to perform jumping jacks in the nude, sit in teammates' urine, and serve as slaves to veterans.

Lengthy articles ran in the *Boston Globe* and the *Watertown Sun*. A number of influential political representatives lent their support to Lenaghan. She also in turn gave her advice and support to Michael DiGiovanni and his parents. Lenaghan formed an antihazing organization called CHORUS (Campus Hazing's Offensive Rituals Undermine Schools) that had some influence upon educator, coach, and student awareness—particularly in eastern Massachusetts.

In the wake of the media attention, Watertown High School suspended three coaches, who all pled ignorance about the hazing traditions, and dropped numerous players from the squad. The head coach, John Barbati, who was suspended for one year, said he thought one of the hazing rituals, a traditional cookie race, involved players using their noses to push a cookie. He said he "never dreamed" the tradition consisted of players running with cookies in their buttocks' cheeks.[9] In time, a sophomore at Medford High School in Massachusetts charged that he too had endured a race with food between his buttocks' cheeks; losers were forced to eat the cookies at the completion of the perverse race.

Lenaghan made it clear in public statements, television appearances, and newspaper interviews that high school hazing needed to be eradicated before fatalities began occurring as they had in colleges. "We send our children to school to learn, not to die," said Lenaghan.[10] Lenaghan may have given other victims of high school athletic hazing courage to come forward.

The next hazing scandal in Massachusetts involved the Wilmington High School football team. Among other allegations were charges that veterans at a weeklong preseason camp had ordered young boys to disrobe, to climb nude into a sleeping bag together, and to dangle objects from their erect penises. The rookies who came forward said they were threatened with physical violence. In the aftermath of the public outcry, a *Boston Globe* writer reported that the coach had said that his seniors had let him down by hazing newcomers in spite of a precamp lecture imploring them to act responsibly. The coach resigned.[11]

SOME REASONS FOR HAZING MISBEHAVIOR IN TEAM SPORTS

Experts in group psychology say that when hazing occurs on high school athletic teams or in college fraternities, prospective members are unlikely to cry foul. For the same reasons that a high school student opposed to drugs may weaken and take a puff of marijuana when pressured by friends, a newcomer may submit to hazing activities he or she thinks are reprehensible. Why? The fear of being thought a deviant is powerful. Researchers report that human beings in groups often say and do things among others they would never do or would do differently when alone.[12]

Certainly, it is true of veterans who passively go along with the team hazers when vile practices take place in the locker room. First, they have been conditioned to accept the hazing because they went through it as rookies. Second, they may rationalize that the hazing they endured was worse than what the new rookies are experiencing. Third, they tell themselves that they are among "good guys"—team leaders, who would never do anything *really* wrong—and so they resist the urge to intervene, even when acts amounting to criminal hazing occur before their eyes. Thus, stalwart team players with no record of getting in trouble end up participating or, at best, standing aside to watch the proceedings, without stepping in. These are the very players the coach probably is counting on to intervene.

At a Pennsylvania football camp in 1989, a sexual assault of a Lyndhurst (New Jersey) High School athlete during an initiation demonstrates how members get paralyzed. In this incident, a student was forced to commit a sexual act while as many as thirty players watched. No coaches were fired and only two upperclassmen were booted off the team.[13]

In another New Jersey hazing incident, somewhat less offensive, senior football players at Holmdel High School in 1989 forced twenty younger players to play a game of Twister in the nude. Surprisingly, some parents of those accused of hazing were furious that the school had disciplined their sons.[14] In 1997, more serious hazing accusations were investigated by Holmdel officials.

Those who conduct hazing activities can have many reasons for being involved in what an outsider would view as vile conduct. They may rationalize that they are the keepers of an unpleasant yet essential team tradition that ensures a winning season. They may consciously or unconsciously be exacting revenge for the hazing they went through. Sadly, in some cases, hazing ringleaders, who are cruel even in noninitiation circumstances and display wild mood swings from amiable to highly aggressive, may be abused at home.[15]

A NATIONALLY COVERED CASE

Perhaps the most widely covered case of high school hazing was an 1993 incident that disrupted the life of sophomore football player Brian Seamons of Sky View High School in Smithfield, Utah. After older teammates stripped Seamons and tied him down in the school's locker room, they added to his humiliation by bringing in a young woman he was dating to witness his degradation.

Seamons sued in U.S. District Court, charging that he had endured a type of sexual discrimination, but the case was thrown out. Judge Dee Benson, however, noted in his ruling that the case appeared to show criminal violations with regard to assault and battery, as well as "public policy issues concerning the proper governance and administration of a public high school." After the victim transferred schools, his parents appeared on *ABC Home Show* and other nationally televised programs to highlight their son's plight.[16]

BLAMING THE VICTIM IN ATHLETIC HAZING

On occasion, college and high school administrators have canceled games—and once, at Kent State University, a whole hockey season—as punishment for team hazing. Inevitably, protests quickly follow from student athletes and the general student body, who sometimes blame the victim. Victims naturally fear retribution or further humiliation, and often transfer schools, as Brian Seamons did.

One such hazed athlete was Anthony Erekat, a member of the Lodi (New Jersey) High School football squad. Erekat was savagely attacked by older players during a 1992 football camp initiation. They chopped his hair and hacked off his ponytail. Worse, they spread feces and peanut butter all over his body during the initiation. He won a settlement but never received an apology from the offending players.[17]

TRYING TO ASSESS BLAME

High school coaches who are reprimanded or lose their jobs for not preventing hazing incidents frequently complain they have been unfairly penalized. They argue they cannot supervise their players at all hours. "I can't control sixty kids, and everything they can possibly do, for twenty-four hours a day," said one Massachusetts football coach whose team was accused of hazing.

Coaches' attitudes toward initiations vary from the many who forbid them to those who see them as a way to achieve team unity or as humorous boys-will-be-boys stunts.

WHEN COACHES START OR ENCOURAGE HAZING

A small but disturbing number of high school athletic hazing cases indicate that state educational departments need to educate coaches as well as students about the dangers of initiation rites.

One coach who took the boys-will-be-boys approach was Michael Tate, who worked as a wrestling coach at Colorado's Meeker High School in 1997. Steven Moore, a physically disabled fifteen-year-old freshman, was stripped, tied with duct tape, and sprayed around the genitals and anus with a medicated spray used to toughen skin around blisters, according to his parents. Players carried the young man to the gym, where the girls' basketball team witnessed his humiliation. The parents said that Tate, the wrestling coach, failed to intervene to stop the ill treatment of their son.[18] Although Tate had been highly successful in winning championships, his teacher's license was revoked in the state of Colorado as punishment.

Soon other troubling stories about Tate came out. According to the *Denver Post,* Tate acknowledged that he had taped the mouth and hands of a talkative thirteen-year-old and left him in the hall. A passing principal found other students taunting the boy, who had been reduced to tears. "The whole class was in on it. It was great fun and I didn't consider it discipline," said Tate. Middle school principal Bushrod White disagreed, replying "You can't humiliate a student and scar him emotionally."[19]

Another disturbing story of unenlightened coaching took place in Arizona. In the March 10, 1999, issue of the *Arizona Republic*, columnist Phil Boas blasted a decision by Gilbert High School to hire a football coach with a history of defending hazing as a psychological motivational tool. Moreover, this coach admitted to actually starting a tradition of letting students punish perceived slackers while he was a coach at another high school. Boas cited an interview that the coach, Jesse Parker, gave to a rival newspaper in defense of practices such as players punishing other players for offenses by administering "pink bellies," occasionally hard enough to cause bleeding. "In our namby-pamby society, people like me are looked at like Neanderthals, but I believe strongly you don't get something for nothing," Parker told the *Tribune*. "If you're going to be the best, you've got to work harder, have more intensity and more determination."[20] Parker, whose teams had won five state championships, divulged that for the pink belly punishment to be effective, it had to be painful, and he admitted that there was a hand-dragging technique that could intensify discomfort.[21]

Jesse Parker said that he had started the pink belly practice when he was a coach at Mesa Mountain View High School in the 1970s. He left the school, but the practice apparently remained. In 1998, the Mesa school board suspended the new head football coach and two assistant coaches briefly for not abolishing the practice started by their predecessor. "This practice is wrong and I won't deny that," suspended head coach Bernie Busken told the *Arizona Republic*. "But we're good people and we love our players."[22]

As might be expected, some state high school football players defended the practice, saying pink belly punishments were no more ludicrous than the sport of football itself, which allows 300-pound (136-kg) players to run full steam into smaller players. "I have had pink bellies that made me bleed," Dallin Pennington, a defensive lineman for one state team said defiantly in a letter to the *Arizona Republic* editor. "I would rather have a pink belly and a state championship than a yellow belly and nothing to show for it."[23]

And while few high school coaches would go on the record to defend this kind of treatment, the fact that so many coaches have hazed and been hazed makes it clear it will take concerted education efforts for old, misguided attitudes about hazing to die out.

ATHLETIC HAZING CONTINUES

Widespread publicity about brutal athletic hazing in high schools has done little to halt it. Here are some recent examples of particularly objectionable athletic initiations.

- In Pinellas County, Florida, five baseball players at Palm Harbor University High School punched and harassed rookies in 1998 on the team bus, putting a burning ointment onto one rookie's bare buttocks.[24]

- In northern Illinois, at Prospect High School, a freshman football player who had been the target of teasing was accosted by teammates in the locker room. Although stories varied dramatically, witnesses said the young man's shorts and underwear had been pulled down. When the case went to trial in 1999, the victim testified that he had been sexually assaulted. The plaintiffs countered that they were indulging in mere horseplay.[25]

- At Thorndale High School in Texas, four football players pleaded guilty to misdemeanor hazing in 1998 for ramming a soda bottle into the victim's anal region. The victim not only quit the junior varsity football team but was also so humiliated that he transferred schools. "These kids [the attackers] have no idea what they've done to my family," the victim's mother told a reporter.[26]

- At Carmel High School in Indiana, the swim team coach was indicted in 1999 for allegedly failing to notify police after a fifteen-year-old member said three other team members sexually violated him in the locker room with an "object," according to the *Indianapolis Star*. The community's swim club came to the coach's defense and blamed the victim in a statement. "[We] are extremely disappointed that an incident which, if it occurred at all, was essentially locker room horseplay and now has been elevated to the level of a criminal issue." According to the *Star*, none of the adult swim club members put their names on the statement.

NATIONAL SURVEY ON ATHLETIC HAZING

The extent of high school athletic hazing can be gleaned from a nationwide survey of 10,000 male and female college athletes conducted by Alfred University with the cooperation of the National Collegiate Athletic Association (NCAA) in 1999. In that survey, eight out of ten athletes said that they had been subjected to initiations. One out of five said their initiation was potentially dangerous, involved alcohol, or met a state statute for criminal hazing.

Of those who said they had been hazed, 42 percent said their first hazing experience occurred in high school and 5 percent said they had been first hazed in middle school. Experts fear that repeated initiations may cause those involved to become desensitized to hazing dangers and degradation.

Chapter Five

HAZING AND ALCOHOL

Tragically, at least one college student has died in alcohol-related sports initiations or pledging stunts every year since 1970. Many high school educators are frantically working on policies that forbid freshman hazing, rookie initiations, and dangerous student club hijinks, hoping to prevent these kinds of hazing deaths from trickling down to high schools.

However, recent newspaper stories show that more needs to be done in the way of hazing and alcohol education programs at the high school level. At Roosevelt High School in Des Moines, Iowa, some students participate in Big Pal, Little Pal, a nonsanctioned autumn tradition in which older students invite new female students to drink with them.[1] Also in Des Moines, at Abraham Lincoln High School, at least one student participated in a life-threatening alcohol-related initiation for a social club with a reputation for heavy partying.[2] And in New Mexico in 1997, a fourteen-year-old Santa Fe High School freshman almost died in an initiation during an event akin to homecoming. Found passed out on a friend's property with a blood-alcohol level of about .30, he didn't return to consciousness until the next day. Someone had scrawled a crude phrase on his condiment-stained clothing and inked "'98" on his head. "We're just thankful that he survived. He was a victim of hazing," the boy's father told a reporter.[3]

Alcohol deaths in college student clubs since the 1970s fall into several categories. Some die from alcohol poisoning or suffocating on their vomit during fraternity initiations that require chugging large amounts of alcohol. Some gulp twenty-one drinks on their twenty-first—and last—birthday. Some fall to their deaths from roofs or while "surfing" atop vehicles. Others climb behind the wheel of a car or trust a drunken student to drive them home. All this occurs even as the general level of alcohol use in the United States drops a little more each year.

After fraternity pledge Jonathan McNamara died at the University of Vermont in an alcohol-related tragedy, his grieving father addressed the state legislature in 1999 to plead for a hazing law and express his disbelief that such stupid, archaic traditions continue. "I at one time belonged to a fraternity," he said. "I had been hazed but that was back in 1966. They don't do the same things that they did to us—do they?"

A PATTERN OF SELF-DESTRUCTION AMONG TEENAGERS

Several recent cases of alcohol poisoning, teen drunk-driving deaths, and arrests of high school fraternity members at drinking parties make educators wonder what has happened to teenagers' judgment and parental supervision.

In February 1999, fifty-six teenagers belonging to a national high school fraternity and three adult chaperones from Mississippi staying in a hotel in Covington, Louisiana, were interviewed by police after dozens of teenagers ended up drunk at a party. The incident upset many city residents. Just six months earlier, a Louisiana State University fraternity had pleaded no contest to eighty-six criminal charges following the alcohol-related death of Benjamin Wynne, a Sigma Alpha Epsilon (SAE) pledge from Covington, during a 1997 marathon drinking bout.[4]

Like many young men who have died in alcohol-related club and fraternal initiations, Wynne first experimented with alcohol in secondary school. Experts on alcohol abuse say that college students often establish destructive drinking patterns in high school or earlier. A survey by the National Institute on Alcohol Abuse and Alcoholism indicates that a whopping 40 percent of the admitted alcoholics they interviewed began drinking before age fifteen. In contrast, a comparatively low 10 percent of those who became alcoholics waited to drink until they were of legal age.

What California educator and pediatrician Charles Irwin notes about teen drinking also applies to teen hazing. "Teens don't see drinking in terms of its negative effects," said Irwin. "Instead, they think something good will happen if they drink; it will improve their self confidence or help their social life."[5]

DRINKING AND ATHLETES

While many college athletes are good students and benefit from participation in sports, in the last decade researchers have discovered that varsity players tend to drink about twice as much as the general student population. Such studies may reveal why initiations often revolve around a rookie's perceived ability to handle alcohol.

With underage drinking an act of rebellion for some teenagers and college students, it is hardly surprising that rookie hazing sometimes requires new players to continue drinking until all alcohol supplied by veterans has been consumed or they pass out. Among college varsity athletes, initiations since 1988 have had scary consequences at Alfred University (on men's football team), Kent State University (on men's hockey team), and Potsdam (New York) State College (on female lacrosse team). Alcohol abuse among male and female athletic teams in Canada is under study by two researchers in Calgary. Alcohol-related initiations have caused severe problems at the University of Western Ontario and other Canadian schools.

THE STORY OF NICK HABEN

The death of rookie athlete Nick Haben, aged eighteen, after a Western Illinois University lacrosse club hazing incident teaches terrible lessons: first, alcohol can kill—anyone—swiftly and painfully; second, risky initiations can go wrong at any time, no matter how long they have been carried out without incident; third, left unchecked, the kind of rampant hazing in colleges that killed Nick Haben will trickle down to high school—the frenzied, one-day high school initiation activities in Des Moines, Iowa, and Santa Fe, New Mexico, mentioned earlier in this chapter will gradually lead to fatalities for high school students.

At Oswego (Illinois) High School, Nick Haben had been a popular young man with athletic ability, good looks, and an eye-to-eye smile. He was also a good student and a member of the National Honor Society. A nondrinker who admitted to tasting two beers once to satisfy his curiosity, Nick was happy to sip soda at parties. A strong catcher and the most valuable player on his high school baseball team, he went to Western Illinois University hoping to play ball, until he learned the team already had six catchers. Instead, he decided to go out for lacrosse, and he made the club.

Nick and his parents had no idea that the lacrosse club was in a kind of free fall, having just come off of a suspension

Nick Haben was eighteen when he died after a sports club initiation in 1990.

after some players had illegally used the team's gas credit card to fill their own automobile tanks. Supervision was abysmal, with an adviser in name only. Since being recruited to the job in 1982, Lowell G. Oxtoby, a heavyset librarian with a love for antiques and Delta Tau Delta, the fraternity he also advises, had served as the club's adviser. But one day, when he came to practice, some of the players mocked him crudely, and he left the field, hurt and bewildered, never to return.

Instead of quitting as adviser and alerting the university, Oxtoby continued to sign authorization slips for travel. He was never aware that veterans initiated the rookies and portrays himself as a victim of team deception. "I didn't know until this incident," says Oxtoby. "It had been kept from me completely. . . . Just as any parent would not know about drinking or smoking behind their backs unless they see evidence of it, because my contact was so minimal there was no way I could detect it."

In an interview several years after Nick's death, his mother, Alice Haben, said she felt Oxtoby's ignorance of the team's collective abuse of alcohol was tantamount to negligence. He hadn't even been aware that the lacrosse club's president had recently resigned over alcohol problems on the team.[6]

Without an adviser, except in name, the team's only supervision was a twenty-one-year-old student coach, Brian Donchez. He was assisted by student officers Daniel Carey, Anthony Kolovitz, Scott Rakita, and Marc Anderson. Anderson later said his title was little more than honorific.

On the field, the lacrosse players loved the game and played hard. Once the game started, the rookie status of the hustling midfielder Haben and the other players was forgotten. Off the field, however, the players, in white team jackets, drank beer after practices and on road trips, leaving the non-drinker Haben to return to his residence hall alone. Because the club's good times revolved around alcohol and Nick's revolved around his friends, classes, family, and church, only a few teammates got to know him, and vice versa.

Soon, Nick and the other rookies began hearing scary stories about the initiation they would have to endure. Although he was frightened by the prospect and intimidated by some of the veterans, Nick began to think seriously about drinking to support his fellow rookies as they tried to pass the inane test of manhood. Nick's cousin, Jason Altenbern, talked to Nick the evening before the scheduled drinking marathon and later described Nick as "scared."[7]

The day of the initiation, veterans broke the hazing into afternoon and evening sessions. The annual team hazing was unplanned and chaotic, much like the club's own relationship with the university and absent faculty adviser. Many of the players were also members of fraternities, where, in spite of a school ban on kegs, young people often passed out from alcohol during parties. For fun, some fraternity members would become instantly intoxicated by "inhaling" liquor through a bong, or water pipe.

On the afternoon of October 18, 1990, the lacrosse initiation began at 3:30 P.M. One of the veterans produced a paddle, delivering a few stinging shots to the behinds of rookies. A couple of veterans laughed uneasily during the paddling for none of them had been paddled as rookies. Three or four veterans proceeded to growl, curse, and taunt the rookies in feigned anger. Nick and the other eight rookies had to strip to their underwear and run onto the women's soccer field to perform odd-looking calisthenics meant to make them look foolish. The rookies were given vodka, though Nick declined to drink any, as well as sips from a pail of a foul concoction called rookie juice, composed of tuna, condiments, pepper sauce, clam or lime juice, a little beer, and some schnapps. According to veteran Marc Anderson, each rookie took only a mouthful or two.

The team was released for dinner. Nick gathered with his fellow rookies before the initiation and drank some olive oil and ate half of a loaf of bread. He had heard somewhere that it was important to coat your stomach before drinking. The team's rookies went back to the practice field for more hazing and to choke down cheap, bad-tasting wine. Veterans inked a different number on each rookie's face, then ordered him to do more calisthenics.

Of course no one can know exactly what was on Nick's mind by this time. Perhaps the couple of sips of alcoholic rookie juice made it harder for him to abstain from drinking more. After performing calisthenics, the team went to the house of veterans Jim Boyer and Steve Kadlec in Macomb. They drank some more while the veterans bombarded them with eggs and rubbed food in their hair.

After washing up at one of the residence halls, the rookies went to a wooded area not far from the practice field. The rookies, under the supervision of a handful of veterans, guzzled alcohol while they participated in a scavenger hunt, displayed the head of a dead squirrel, and leaped over a campfire into a nearby river.[8] The veterans, drunk and glassy eyed, were surprised by Nick, the perennial abstainer, who joined the rookies in the swilling of an astonishing amount of tequila, whiskey, gin, vodka, vermouth, beer, and cheap wine. Because the only benchmark available to Nick that night was alcohol consumption, his actions probably reflected his desire to show the veterans his commitment and loyalty to the team, which was so great that he put aside his usual reservations about liquor.

When at last veteran John Bilenko—a young man who says his attitudes about alcohol were formed by images of his father drinking occasionally hard in social situations— finally yanked a bottle of tequila from Nick, it was way too late to keep him from falling into a coma. Some fluid spilled from Nick's lips and he keeled over. Instead of panicking or calling 911, the veterans, determined to finish the initiation, put the rest of the rookies through silly stunts and delivered pep talks about how the lacrosse team had been one of their most important college experiences. No one was worried about the teammate passed out on the ground. Every one of them had seen people pass out before, and everyone expected at least another one to pass out before the initiation was over. "Before we heard Nick was dead it was one of the best times I ever had," said Anderson. "The night was fun. I'm glad I had the experience, the brotherhood, the bonding."

Predictably, newspaper editorials summed up Nick's death as a failure to resist peer pressure. Few commentators were perceptive enough to analyze how sports, alcohol abuse, and hazing had become so intertwined in high school and collegiate life. The press also tended to be judgmental, portraying the lacrosse veterans as full-blown villains instead of students who had somehow gotten through high school and college with little knowledge about the complexities of group behavior.

A TERRIBLE VISIT

The next morning Alice Haben was at her job as church secretary, finishing some arrangements for the trip that she, her husband Dale, and teenage son Charles were taking to Macomb that very weekend. Two policemen entered the building a little after 10 A.M. to speak with Reverend Philip M. Dripps in his office. He came out, gathered himself, and broke Alice Haben's heart in a few bleak sentences. Nick had been found dead on the dormitory room floor of a lacrosse team veteran. A coroner would do an autopsy that afternoon.

No one from the university phoned with details, according to Alice Haben. She had to rely on the coroner and a family relation who worked at the college to find out about Nick's last hours.[9]

At first, after hearing the reverend's news, Alice had a moment of hope. Knowing that Nick didn't drink, she conjectured that the victim must have stolen her son's identification. But the coroner confirmed that Nick had indeed been the young man who had died from drinking at a party or some sort of initiation. In a fog, Alice went home to break the news to her husband and son, and then made arrangements for Nick's body to be brought back to Oswego for a Sunday funeral.

On Saturday, after hundreds of relatives, friends, and strangers had come to the funeral parlor, Alice and Dale Haben brought Nick's high school friends home. They sat with Charles, telling him story after story that brought his older brother to life again.

"It's 1 A.M.," a relative complained to Alice. "They have to go home."

"No," she said. "They don't."

THE LACROSSE CLUB'S REACTION

Nick's death had little impact on the drinking habits of students at Western Illinois University. During the month after his death, two more students suffered from alcohol poisoning but survived. None of the lacrosse players thought they would be welcome at the wake, and that knowledge agonized the more sensitive members of the team. A few more hardened members rationalized that it had been the rookie's fault for breaking his own vow not to drink. But veteran Mark Molzer disagreed and addressed the team in a meeting two days after the burial, saying "We've gone too far."

When the lacrosse players walked on campus, voices grew quiet and then loud. "Killers," one student whispered to a passing veteran.

Oxtoby, the club's absentee adviser, was also distraught. "A young man is dead," said Oxtoby. "Who knows, he might have been president of the United States. He might have been a doctor, and certainly he had a soul." If Oxtoby had refused to sign vouchers for travel money and forced the team to shape up, close down, or get a new adviser, a death might have been prevented, as Nick's mother learned from depositions, private investigations, and police reports. As a member of the Delta Tau Delta fraternity, Oxtoby knew about hazing. During the 1980s, one of the country's leading hazing experts and author of a study condemning hazing, Dr. Frederick D. Kershner, was a member of Oxtoby's own fraternity.

A SEARCH FOR ANSWERS

Soon after the funeral the Habens pieced together the last minutes of their son's life from conversations—in which the word "hazing" surfaced now and again—and from a private investigator whom the family hired to re-create Nick's last day. Alice Haben learned that veterans and rookies had taken Nick's still body to the room of Anthony Kolovitz and Andrew Reese in Henninger Hall. A Western Illinois University resident adviser named Michael P. Reimann, a paid employee of the university, helped prop a cushion under Nick—apparently for protection from suffocation in case he vomited—and left him alone without calling for medical assistance or reporting the incident to the police.

Incredibly, as Nick lay gurgling, Kolovitz came back at 2:30 A.M. and went into a lounge to sleep. Reese came back late too, awoke early in the morning, heard Nick wheezing, went to the bathroom for water, and fell back to sleep. The two could be called insensitive, but thousands of college students might also have failed to identify the situation as a crisis.

Sometime after 8 A.M., Reese noticed that Nick's face and body had turned purple from a lack of oxygen. Now in a panic, he summoned Kolovitz. Instead of phoning police, the two phoned other lacrosse veterans to find out what to do. One player advised them to call the authorities and an ambulance.

They waited too long: Nick died right in front of them. By the time the police arrived, rigor mortis had already stiffened Nick's body. His blood-alcohol content was .34.

Frightened and upset, Reese and Kolovitz told a police officer that Nick had passed out at a party. Not until about two hours later when Nick's resident adviser talked to campus police did the officers have any idea that a hazing incident had taken place.

A thorough and professional investigation by the university police followed, with the suspension or expulsion of twelve players. The action prompted an angry letter from Barbara Rokita, mother of one lacrosse veteran, to the Western Illinois University student newspaper, accusing the university of turning its back on the team. "These boys have lost a friend and cannot even grieve for him," she wrote. "They are so consumed with fear, anger, confusion and pain."

A CONTROVERSIAL COURT CASE

Days after her son's funeral, Alice Haben happened to turn on the television and see a CNN program about hazing. Information about the organization called CHUCK flashed on the screen. Alice Haben called one of the show's guests, Eileen Stevens, who listened to her plight, sent related literature, and gave her a crash course on hazing. Reverend Dripps put the family in touch with Robert C. Strodel, a respected author and attorney from Peoria, Illinois, who agreed to explore the possibility of pressing criminal or civil charges.

"Is there any justification for such a cruel and barbaric practice?" Reverend Dripps wrote about hazing in his United Methodist Church newsletter. "We simply cannot stand by and allow the present situation to continue unabated or unchallenged. . . . A new climate of civility and reason needs to be created not only in our colleges and universities but also in our home communities. This will not be an easy task. The forces of evil and indifference will no doubt combine to stave off such efforts to dissolve the practice of hazing."

The Habens' case against the lacrosse team was shaky, according to the judge who first heard the case. Illinois's hazing law was ninety years old, and the judge concurred with the team members' attorneys, who attacked its language.

In response, the state's attorney of McDonough County, William Poncin, visited the Haben house and listened carefully to Alice Haben, who argued against putting the young men in jail with hardened criminals and for making the point that hazing and underage drinking are a deadly combination. She wanted rookies and pledges to know they had the right to refuse to participate in hazings. She wanted older members to know they would be held accountable if they broke the law and hazed. "We weren't out for revenge," said Alice Haben. "We wanted to correct a problem."

Years and many court hearings came and went. Alice Haben, guided by the unflappable Poncin and supported by dozens of Oswego neighbors, won at last: the Illinois Supreme Court upheld the old state hazing law and the twelve lacrosse veterans were put on trial. They were convicted not on the charge of hazing but of serving alcohol to a minor. Judge Larry Heiser was mindful of the impact of conviction on the lives of the defendants—young men who had not intended to hurt their friend and had been prosecuted for actions that hundreds of thousands of other college students had done without consequence.

"At the time it happened I thought we pretty much were scapegoats," said Anderson, who believed the university should have carried out a full-blown investigation of hazing instead of banishing those involved. "The problem is not just us, and the problem is a big problem."

Judge Heiser gave the defendants community service assignments and ordered them to tell their story to the author of this book. If they complied with court supervision, the charges would eventually be expunged from their records. Most of the young men carried out the judge's order and made this very chapter possible. Others, such as the student coach Brian Donchez, refused to get in touch, perhaps on the advice of their attorneys. Anderson and Molzer apologized to Alice Haben individually, and she wrapped her arms around them both. "We lost a friend that evening," Molzer later said. "I feel terrible about it."

The Habens then settled with eleven of the twelve defendants for a total of $530,000, after dropping one young man whose family had no insurance. The Western Illinois University student newspaper criticized the judgment, saying Nick "was ultimately responsible for his own demise." The columnist wrote, "In an effort to assign blame for the loss of their son the Habens are ruining the lives of twelve people who are a lot like their son: young, naive and mired in the need to be a part of something at any cost."[10]

Defendant Marc Anderson disagreed with the paper and condemned press coverage for not investigating the widespread hazing problem. He sometimes imagines his own mother's reaction if he had died instead of Nick. "Ethically, should I have had sense enough to realize that it's not normal to be in the condition [Nick] was in?" Anderson asked himself. He still wrestles with that question and the consequences of the event—which in his mind have dashed his dream of one day becoming governor of Illinois. Anderson stresses that the trial made him look hard into his own soul and "has made me a better person."

The trial over, Alice Haben says she hopes one clear message was sent to the high school and college youth of

America: "If it's not a positive initiation, if it's not going to help someone, [you] have no business doing it." She adds, "The decision to have an initiation should not be left up to students any more than they should decide whether to drink and drive."

AFTERMATH

Alice Haben eventually left her job at the church but continues to visit any high school interested in hearing her speak about hazing. With William Poncin, she lobbied for a tougher Illinois hazing law and enlisted the aid of her state representative from Oswego. In 1996, a law that includes provisions for felony hazing was passed, and Illinois governor Jim Edgar approved a measure permitting prosecutors the option of seeking a three-year prison term in hazing incidents that result in severe injuries or death.

"If you can make anything positive out of what's happened to her son, I think she has in creating a hazing awareness movement," Poncin said in a recent interview.

Now and then Alice Haben walks over to Nick's old high school. Oswego High School renamed its baseball Most Valuable Player Award the Nick Haben Award and erected a trophy case in his memory. At the top of a wood plaque, above Nick's picture, is an inscription from hazing activist Eileen Stevens: "Let us always remember the true meaning of brotherhood—a fellowship: an interaction between individuals sharing the same goals, ideals and principles. Never let that camaraderie be blemished by apathy or any form of indifference or abuse. Continue to work together, learn together and care for each other."

High school drinking in *Dazed and Confused*

ALCOHOL AND HAZING IN HOLLYWOOD FILMS

Hollywood movies about high school hazing, especially the 1993 cult hit *Dazed and Confused*, may serve as a challenge to teenagers, giving them a kind of benchmark for how far to take their hazing. In fact, in a 1998 incident, two of the three Williamsville (Illinois) High School males accused of paddling seven freshman boys with a shop-made paddle said they were inspired by scenes of hazing in *Dazed and Confused*.[11]

For college fraternity males, the movie *Animal House* serves a similar purpose, providing a rationalization for hazing. Phi Gamma Delta pledge

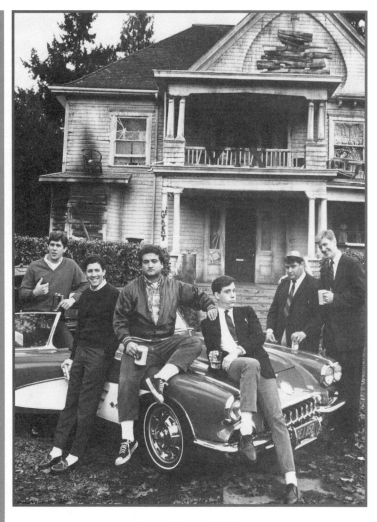

Fraternity members in *Animal House* (1979)

Scott Krueger at Cambridge's Massachusetts Institute of Technology (MIT) in 1997 was shown that film before beginning the breakneck drinking rituals that put him in a coma and then ended his life.

Both *Dazed and Confused* and *Animal House* depict drinking and hazing as cool, exciting things for young people to do. *Dazed and Confused*, a cult video favorite that spent twenty-three weeks on a video best-seller list in 1993, may lead students to conclude that initiations are a vital part of their entrance into high school and high school organizations or teams.

While these movies cannot be solely blamed for the rise in teen drinking and hazing, neither can their influence on susceptible young viewers be totally dismissed.[12]

Chapter Six

GANG INITIATIONS

Experts on delinquency agree that providing a precise definition of "gang" is difficult. In this book the term refers to loosely or tightly knit organizations of young males and/or, to a lesser extent, females, involved in antisocial, rebellious, or illegal behavior. This chapter concentrates on gang hazing in high school, although members can be elementary school age or adult. While gangs in the late 1960s and early 1970s were mainly based in metropolitan areas, criminal activity by gangs in the 1990s became a growing problem in suburbia and even in small, remote towns.

To outsiders, all gangs may look alike, but anyone studying them closely finds stark differences. Gangs will often have different political views, positions in the community, levels of cooperation with rival gangs, and may even develop philosophic views toward society.

Some gangs are small and disorganized. Some integrate members of various races. Some gangs are regularly involved in criminal activities. Some occasionally participate benevolently in community involvement, particularly to help younger children in their neighborhood, though critics argue it is merely a recruiting ploy. Some run illegal drug operations with the skill of entrepreneurs, which gives members local status. Some are profitable, giving leaders access to cars, guns, and cash. Many use sports as a way to relax and exercise, while others see sports as just another form of income—gambling on neighborhood basketball games, for example.

Most members have dreams of improving their lot in life. A few gang members will take opportunities provided by social service agencies, universities, and well-run community centers to renounce gang membership and even to work with former gang members to give them alternatives, hope, and connections to employment opportunities. Sometimes these include young women whose association with gang members has made them into young mothers with many responsibilities and little male or family support.[1]

ALL IN THE FAMILY

Significantly, teenage members of gangs say that their satisfaction in belonging is that they feel part of a family. In many cases, they come from single-parent or single-guardian homes. These young people are often left alone at home. If the father is no longer in the home or is absent for long periods, the young male gang member will often try to model himself after an older gang member and form a relationship with him. Occasionally that model is also a relative. In some cases, gang and family are one, with an uncle and nephew sharing gang membership.

Many gangs also have symbols that express the gang's professed values and kinship. The Vice Lords of Bluffton,

Members often feel closer bonds to their gangs than to their families.

Indiana, a small-city gang dangerous enough to be connected with one slaying, uses a star as its symbol, with the five points representing truth, love, peace, justice, and freedom.[2]

Gangs have descriptive names for both the group and each individual. Some names reflect the gang's turf, as in the 38th Street Gang in Los Angeles or the St. Louis West End Boyz. A few gangs found in major cities and small towns across the nation, such as the Crips, are the McDonald's of the gang world; for them, expansion translates into huge profits from drug marketing.

Given the gang squabbles over power and drugs that have killed so many members during the last three decades, there is no question that prospective members trade their dysfunctional family at home for an equally addictive dysfunctional extended family when they accept a beating to join. The cost of the empathy and caring of others is expensive once a member gets involved in criminal activities with a gang.

Opportunities for young people to escape their environment diminish after they join gangs, particularly if they get felony records. Even if they stay out of trouble, employers are rarely impressed with their gang tattoos. The benefits of teenage gang membership, in other words, are short term and insufficient, given the risks, hardships, and potential criminal punishment.

NONMEMBER VICTIMS

Gangs operate in thousands of junior high schools and high schools in the United States. Initiation beatings of new members often take place on school property. Schools beset with gangs also face problems with nonmembers being harassed, victimized, and sometimes even murdered.

In 1993, two Houston, Texas, teenaged girls inadvertently walked into a gang initiation. The mistake cost them their lives. At their drinking hangout near a set of railroad tracks, six members of the Black N White Gang were about to beat two young initiates when Elizabeth Pena, aged sixteen, and Jennifer Ertman, aged fourteen, surprised the group. Pena and Ertman were heading home but never got there. Gang members began sexually attacking the girls, causing the two prospective members to flee without trying to help. The six gang members—one juvenile and five adults—viciously raped the two passersby, strangled them, and defiled their corpses.[3]

Another problem for educators and police is when non-gang members are killed by gang members in cases of mistaken identity. The innocent have died because they unintentionally made a gesture or wore a symbolic color of clothing mistakenly taken as disrespectful of the gang. Brenda Harris, aged seventeen, paid a terrible price for waving out a car window. Gang members Darrell Massey and Gregory Smith mistook her gesture, pursued the car, and sprayed it with bullets, killing her.[4]

"JUMP-INS" OR "BEAT-INS" FOR OUTSIDERS

Gangs sometimes allow uninitiated people, or outsiders, to associate with them if they provide some sort of limited service to the group. For example, the outsiders may have a drug connection, loan vehicles, or perform some sort of servile function. Others may be younger than most gang members and in time will be expected to undergo an initiation to join.

The presence of "wanna-be" outsiders reinforces the perception for gang members that their group has value. The fact that there are outsiders obviously hungry for membership is taken by gang members to mean that the uninitiated are unworthy, undesirable, and expendable.

But when someone wants to become a member, and the gang agrees to it, a common initiation ritual is a bloody beating, called a jump-in, a beat-in, and other slang terms.

To join a gang, prospective members must often submit to a beating.

Simply stated, the initiate takes on multiple gang members with no hope of winning. The initiate must prove to the gang that he or she possesses courage, toughness, and a desire to belong.

One typical rule for a jump-in is that the prospective member must endure the beating for a set amount of time. New members must show that they can take a pounding. The initiation convinces members that a prospective member really wants to join, is fit to be trusted in a violent confrontation with a rival gang, and is likely to participate in all of the gang's violent and criminal activities.

At age fourteen, Luis Rodriguez, author of *Always Running, Gang Days in L.A.*, endured a savage initiation by adult males in a Latino gang, which could have left him dead or paralyzed. Today, beatings are required for initiations into big-city gangs. They have also occurred in places with relatively low crime rates, such as Chattanooga, Tennessee, and Washington's Yakima Valley.

Sometimes potential members have the desire but not the good luck to get through a beating. Jerry Wager, a thirteen-year-old runaway, approached three gang members drinking beer on school property at Fairview Junior High School in the state of Washington. According to them, he asked to be beaten for admission to the gang and they complied. Not only did the one adult and two juveniles beat the young boy, but they also stuffed a paper sack into his mouth. He died of suffocation.[5]

BEATINGS AS GANG RITUAL

Many outsiders naturally question how so many young people can be so eager to endure such brutal rituals to join a group. Rosalind Miles, an author who studies behavior in males, compares gang initiations with the painful initiations of primitive societies whose purpose "is to burn into each boy's mind the folk memory of the key myths and values of the tribe."[6] Having taken a beating from other gang members who have endured the same beating, the newcomer gains a bond closer than he has with family members, particularly if they are absent or otherwise unreliable, says Miles.

Most importantly, by keeping his face impenetrable during the beating, by masking whatever fear is deep within, the initiate manages to convince the other gang members that he is a fit fellow warrior—someone they can take into rival gang territories with them.

"You could never risk your neck outside your street by yourself, without the other guys," said a former Harlem gang member. "Man, you'd be . . . crazy even to think it, you'd be caught, beaten to a pulp, dead. You weren't in a gang, you weren't *nobody*. But to be in was war, just war; you'd never believe the violence, knives, bricks, broken glass. I was so terrified, but I never dared show it. If you showed yourself to be a coward, your life wasn't worth dog-do."[7]

The act of fighting has little negative stigma in the communities from which some prospective members hail. Indeed, an ability to win fights gains admiration and even respect from others, and individuals manage to grab back a bit of self-esteem that has sometimes been lost after much failure in school. In addition, in time the gang member can easily perceive teachers and police as aggressors "out to get him."[8]

As many sociologists have pointed out, a predisposition for gang life really starts in a member's early, unsupervised childhood, when he or she learns survival skills in unruly play groups controlled by the strongest, most aggressive playmates. For many individuals, such play is anything but fun. Miles writes that the boy "who fails to find meaning through play . . . begins, even at the youngest age, to turn to crime and violent activity to fill the void." She cites an observation by New York psychologist Shawn Johnson that may explain why some gang members startled him by recalling their initiation beatings with zest and pride. "These children are dead inside," says Johnson. "For them to feel alive and important they have to engage in some terrible sadistic activity."[9]

Many neighborhoods also introduce their young to predator gangs from other neighborhoods, forcing individuals into gang units for mutual protection and social interaction. The community also offers gang members buyers for stolen goods and illicit drugs.[10]

Gang members want protection and assurances that the new members can protect their backs during clashes with rival gangs. There is also a perception here, as with some college fraternities and high school clubs, that a tougher initiation is symbolic of a tougher, higher-status group.

OTHER GANG INITIATION RITUALS

Some gangs have other initiation rituals. They may ask prospective members to steal for them or to procure cigarettes, drugs, and alcohol. Gang members may require a gang tattoo, signifying lifelong membership and ruining initiates' opportunities for military service, where gang tattoos are forbidden.

Initiates may be put in danger zones out of the gang's turf. Members drop them off in the territory of a rival gang with a can of spray paint. The initiates must show bravery by putting up graffiti that lets the rivals know their territory has been invaded. Ultraviolent gangs can ask new members to hurt another gang member or an innocent third party as a way of showing loyalty.

In one instance, the alert action of a gas station attendant in South Stockton, California, saved the life of Susanna Jones. The attendant spotted a male intruder getting into the back seat of Jones's car and summoned police. A sixteen-year-old boy told the officers who apprehended him that he was under orders to rape and kill a woman that night to prove himself worthy of membership in his chosen gang.[11]

Girls who join gangs generally have little choice about the initiation requirement, which is to get "sexed in," or initiated by having sexual relations with members. Occasionally, small city gangs will offer young women the option of a timed beating from multiple members.[12]

TWO STANDARDS OF JUSTICE

Not all students involved in beatings join gangs out of choice. Often, young people who have the potential to serve the gang well or raise its status are forced to accept an initiation beating.

Students expelled from school for taking part in gang initiations rarely have the clout to get help from administrators and school boards. This is especially true if the authorities discovered the initiation in progress on school property. For example, in Florida, after two Leesburg High School students and one Oak Park Middle School student were caught performing a gang initiation rite in 1996 on a school athletic field, they were quickly expelled by the Lake

County school board.[13] Those expelled for gang hazing are unlikely to show up at the next school meeting with an attorney carrying subpoenas, as happens occasionally when athletes get bounced for hazing.

COSTS OF GANG MEMBERSHIP

Even if high school athletes conduct an initiation that is violent or involves underage drinking, school officials often try to handle it as an internal problem. Police seldom intervene unless an injury occurs or the victim hazed complains or threatens to sue. On the other hand, administrators frequently call for police assistance when gang initiations happen on school property. For example, in September 1996, after allegations surfaced that five teen and preteen boys from Falls Church, Virginia, had beaten a thirteen-year-old boy as part of a gang initiation, administrators from Glasgow Intermediate School quickly turned the matter over to the Fairfax County police.[14]

Although gang members are seldom interested in the hard work needed to earn a high school diploma, many of them keep their gang affiliations quiet to stay in school as long as possible. Some have family pressures to stay in school. Some want access to members of the opposite sex. Others use their time in school to arrange drug transactions or steal from classmates or teachers. Occasionally, some form attachments with nongang friends and teachers that in time inspire them to contemplate a fresh start outside the gang.

EFFECTS OF GANG RITUALS ON FRATERNITIES

One possible consequence of gang members staying in school is inadvertently introducing the practice of beatings as an initiation ritual into the ranks of some high school social clubs and college Greek-letter groups, particularly historically African-American fraternities. While all African-American national fraternities officially ban rough physical initiations, they have thus far failed to persuade many undergraduate and graduate members to shun violent initiation rituals. The result has been the beating-related deaths of Joel Harris at Morehouse College, Michael Davis at Southeast Missouri State, and Vann Watts at Tennessee State University, plus dozens of serious injuries ranging from damaged kidneys to broken bones. Many African-American members get their Greek letters branded on their skin with a coat hanger, mimicking the practice of gangs such as the Gangster Disciples, which also use a hanger to brand letters and symbols into the flesh of members.[15]

QUITTING A GANG

According to three experts on gang behavior, Rick Landre, Mike Miller, and Dee Porter, leaving a gang means that a member must endure a final, no-holds-barred beating, plus the possibility that their family may suffer retribution. Even then, the person who wants to walk away may not be permitted to if he violates a rule such as getting knocked unconscious. According to their research, members rejecting the gang lifestyle have been killed or suffered permanent injuries. The threat to life is so real that some experts who work with gangs find it more prudent to steer an entire gang into a sociably acceptable lifestyle than to ask an individual to risk all by quitting the gang.

Even incarceration fails to stop some gang members. When put in jail, the prisoners join prison gangs or initiate other prisoners, allowing them to wear the old gang's colors.[16] Several inmates have died as a result of prison initiations in which potential gang members are required to kill a prisoner, occasionally of a specific race.

Chapter Seven

HAZING AND THE LAW

In May 1999, Eileen Stevens stepped onstage with graduating seniors in front of the Alfred University faculty. Unlike the other dark-robed recipients, Eileen Stevens had never taken a course at the university. She was present to accept an honorary degree for her work as an antihazing activist. Her son, Chuck Stenzel, died the first night of pledging during an alcohol-related initiation in the nearby Klan Alpine fraternity house in 1978.

The night Chuck died, fraternity members pressured all the pledges to drink. As part of a bewildering mental game, they took each young man aside and told him he had been rejected. Crushed and humiliated, each pledge was given a bottle of liquor and taken on a ride in the trunk of a car. More drinking games followed. The party theme was "Don't Stop until You Drop." The Klan

Alpine members liked Chuck and thought he would sleep off the liquor as most of them had done as pledges. By 11:30 P.M., however, Chuck Stenzel was dead, his mother's heart shattered with a call from the school's dean of students in the middle of the night.

Chuck Stenzel's autopsy revealed a blood-alcohol content of .46; he had downed the rough equivalent of about two dozen drinks of wine, whiskey, and beer in a very short period of time. The emergency medical team called to the Klan Alpine fraternity house could not save him. That night, two other pledgemates of Chuck's almost died and owe their lives to local emergency and hospital personnel.

Of course, the young men of Klan Alpine—serious students by day and drinkers by night—never intended to harm Chuck or the other pledges. After his death, some members were ashamed and some defiantly blamed the victim for his participation. At that time, no hazing laws that made victim consent irrelevant yet existed. After all, pledges and other initiates have no way of giving fully informed consent, particularly under the influence of dangerous amounts of alcohol, to whatever trials and stunts they may be asked to undergo.

"Not all risk-taking is really adventurous," states New York child psychiatrist Beatrix A. Hamburg. "Sometimes it is risk-avoidant to take a drink, smoke a joint, or have sex rather than be ridiculed, shunned or deprecated by peers."[1]

NO PUNISHMENT FOR HAZERS

The honorary degree, called an act of reconciliation by university president Edward Coll, was a far cry from the university's original response—a half-hearted effort to punish the Klan Alpine hazers who had coaxed Chuck, a light drinker, into their alcohol rituals.

Back in 1978, in an attempt at justice, Eileen Stevens turned to New York law enforcement authorities, only to find no hazing law existed. Although the then-district attorney of Allegany County promised an investigation, he

After the death of her son in a hazing incident at Alfred University, Eileen Stevens fought for antihazing legislature nationwide. In 1999, she received an honorary degree for her work from Alfred University president Edward Coll, who called the occasion "bittersweet."

failed to interview the relevant Klan Alpine members and a former adviser who had been one of the first on the scene. The attorney didn't even talk to the state trooper who had tried to restore order in the fraternity house as rescuers searched every closet for other passed-out pledges. In time, even the file containing the investigation notes was taken right out of Allegany County's records storage room.

In short, Eileen Stevens's case fell through the legal cracks. Everyone was sorry, but without a state law in place no one could be held accountable.

THE BATTLE TO GET STATE HAZING LAWS ON THE BOOKS

After founding the Committee to Halt Useless College Killings, or CHUCK, Eileen Stevens uncovered a staggering fact: only a handful of states had hazing laws, and those that did, such as North Carolina and Illinois, were terribly outdated and ambiguously worded.

Determined to change things, Eileen Stevens began visiting libraries and hired a research service to do a computer-assisted search for newspaper articles related to hazing. She found many other hazing deaths with no civil or criminal legal consequences. For example, in 1970, when sorority member Donna Bedinger was kidnapped by pledges at Eastern Illinois University and was killed trying to stop the car from abandoning her in the countryside, the case was ruled an accident. When four pledges from Grove City College in Pennsylvania were hit by a car during a forced march along a highway, authorities regarded the incident as an accident, though they did take some internal steps to prevent a recurrence. When William Flowers, a Zeta Beta Tau pledge from Monmouth College in New Jersey, died of suffocation after being forced to dig and climb into his own grave, which then collapsed on him, the fraternity members considered the death a terrible accident. After initiate John Davies died in a drunken Sundowner club initiation in 1975 at the University of Nevada, his parents were horrified when a grand jury ruled that the club members were morally, but not legally, responsible.

Over the next twenty years, Eileen Stevens began to hear from reporters, parents, and fraternity leaders about dozens of fraternity pledges who had died in hazings, alcohol chugging incidents, birthday celebrations, falls from fraternity house and dormitory roofs, and automobile wrecks. She got phone calls from bereft parents and siblings, including the mothers of William Flowers and John Davies. She heard from Joan Cerra, the mother of a pledge who died at University of Wisconsin; Ray and Maisie Ballou, the parents of University of South Carolina pledge Barry Ballou, who died in his sleep of alcohol poisoning following a hazing; and Adrienne Harris, whose son died in a pledging beating at Morehouse College. She even began hearing from remorseful former hazers, asking how they might help her antihazing campaign. One New Jersey college sociology professor and an older Klan Alpine member, Richard Sigal, started teaching the dangers of hazing and alcohol misuse in related courses.

THE RISE OF ANTIHAZING ACTIVISTS IN GREEK-LETTER GROUPS

By 1990, the ever-rising number of fraternity-related deaths from hazing and alcohol spurred a number of national fraternity and sorority leaders and undergraduates to add their own voices to those of advocates in an attempt to keep friends from killing friends. The Greek-letter society advo-

After Barry Ballou died in a fraternity hazing incident, his parents Ray and Maisie Ballou worked to pass a law banning college hazing in South Carolina. The state legislature later also made high school hazing a criminal matter.

cates included Jonathan Brant, Frank Ruck, and Frederick Kershner of the National Interfraternity Conference (NIC); Maureen Syring, Jean W. Scott, and Lissa Bradford of the National Panhellenic Conference (NPC); and Michael V. W. Gordon of the National Pan-Hellenic Council (NPHC). The NIC, NPC, and NPHC are umbrella organizations that represent national fraternities and sororities, including historically African-American groups.

A few national fraternity executives were drawn into the antihazing movement after receiving unfavorable press coverage for hazing or being sued by the families of hazing victims. Sigma Phi Epsilon, Sigma Nu, Theta Chi, Phi Delta Theta, and Sigma Alpha Epsilon took the strongest stands against hazing after suffering humiliating media exposure concerning hazing incidents in their organizations. In 1990, the leaders of all historically African-American Greek-letter fraternities and sororities dropped pledging, saying that the cruel hazing that had crept into pledging was an affront to the groups' founders.

A NEW PROBLEM: SOME GREEK-LETTER UNDERGRADUATES VERSUS NATIONAL LEADERSHIP

Unfortunately, as the national leadership of many Greek-letter groups work to enforce stricter hazing and alcohol policies, some undergraduate chapter members are revolting. In 1997, the Clarkson University chapter of Theta Chi ignored its national leadership's policies and threw a drunken revelry that lead to the death of seventeen-year-old pledge Binaya "Bini" Oja. Two years later, the fraternity's national leader, Dave Westol, found himself embroiled in a civil suit after Oja's family sued the Theta Chi chapter house and individual fraternity members for damages.

In short, a major challenge for Greek-letter leaders is dealing with secret or "underground" hazing. National leaders of African-American fraternities and sororities threw up their hands in the 1990s as evidence of savage pledge beatings was found at Kansas State University, Indiana University, University of Maryland at College Park and Eastern Shore, and the University of South Florida.

Many college fraternity advisers and a handful of college presidents joined the antihazing and antibinge-drinking activists. A national organization called Security on Campus began monitoring all campus deaths and acts of violence, including those involving hazing. An organization of antihazing students, graduate students, and supporters called the Multi-Jurisdictional Task Force, or the MJTF, which is on the web as StopHazing.org, lobbies in many states for antihazing laws.

HIGH SCHOOL ANTIHAZING ACTIVITIES

Unfortunately, the number of antihazing activists working to prevent high school hazing is small compared to the number of college antihazing activists. Of course, many college antihazing activists work to prevent hazing at all levels, including Eileen Stevens, Alice Haben in Illinois, Mary Lenaghan in Massachusetts, the husband-wife team of Brian Rahill and Elizabeth Allen in Ohio, Rita Saucier, whose son Chad died as a result of pledge drinking at Auburn University in Alabama, and Edith Davis, whose son Michael died after he was beaten as an initiate at a historically African-American fraternity in Missouri.

Only two activists have fought hazing primarily at the high school level. One was sixteen-year-old Nikki Cosentino, who with her mother fought to pass a Minnesota antihazing statute in 1997 after a disturbing hazing incident at her high school. The second was a fifteen-year-old girl who, in the spring of 1999, astounded Vermont state legislators and the governor with her impassioned plea for antihazing legislation after enduring a traumatic high school hazing that required her to simulate a sex act. The student's parents testified, as did Robert McNamara, the father of a seventeen-year-old University of Vermont freshman who perished in a fall from a cliff during a 1992

Chad Saucier, posing here with his sisters in his last family photo, died of alcohol poisoning while pledging at an Auburn University fraternity.

fraternity outdoor ritual in which alcohol was served to minors. The parents of Brian Seamons, the young football player from Utah who sued his teammates for sexual discrimination, also spoke out occasionally against high school hazing, but they eventually grew tired of media intrusions and now decline requests for press interviews.

The lack of advocates at the high school level has a number of causes. First, although high school hazings have caused emotional wounds, alcohol overdoses, sexual trauma, and physical injuries, they have not, thus far, caused the mounting fatalities seen in college hazing. Second, while deplorable high school hazings in Idaho, Vermont, and South Carolina have caused local uproars, they haven't come close to getting the national media attention that incidents at the University of Texas, the Massachusetts

Institute of Technology, Louisiana State University, Southeast Missouri State, and other colleges have received. Third, few school board members and principals have agreed to be interviewed in connection to hazing scandals, and none of them made national pleas for hazing reforms as Theta Chi's Dave Westol, Alfred University's Edward Coll, and Auburn University president William Muse have done.

In East Lansing, Michigan, one superintendent of schools, Jon Reynolds, handled a swim team hazing incident to the satisfaction of a parent who complained, but he now fears outlining hazing offenses with students in advance. He believes such a policy might inspire some students to haze.

Yet as hazing awareness spreads, more and more high schools have thought it prudent to publish strict no-tolerance policies against hazing. However, no high school educator has matched Nikki Cosentino's initiative and become a national spokesperson against hazing.

STATES WITH ANTIHAZING STATUTES

After an initially draining battle, Eileen Stevens and her congressman successfully lobbied New York state legislators to enact an antihazing law. At first the then-governor of New York planned to veto the bill, but another hazing death in the state, this time at Ithaca College, swayed public opinion in Eileen Stevens's favor.

After that law was passed, she testified in hearings for laws in other states, photocopying stacks of newspaper clippings to send to antihazing advocates. Eileen Stevens personally testified in thirteen states. One by one, state laws against hazing began passing. By the end of 1999, laws were passed in Alabama, Arkansas, California, Colorado, Connecticut, Delaware, Florida, Georgia, Idaho, Illinois, Indiana, Iowa, Kansas, Kentucky, Louisiana, Maine, Maryland, Massachusetts, Minnesota, Mississippi, Missouri, Nebraska, Nevada, New Hampshire, New Jersey, New York, North Carolina, North Dakota, Ohio, Oklahoma, Oregon, Pennsylvania, Rhode Island, South Carolina, Tennessee, Texas, Utah, Virginia, Washington, West Virginia, and Wisconsin.

Activists and sympathetic legislators in Vermont hope that they too will succeed in getting hazing statutes passed. Many of the activists who fought to get laws passed in Colorado and Nevada were college students. A large number of them belonged to fraternities and sororities and were unequivocally opposed to hazing. Eileen Stevens has said that the efforts of Greek-letter students and victims of hazing were instrumental in the passage of laws in New Jersey and Maryland.

Once a law is passed, activists sometimes lobby to get state legislators to add amendments that eliminate loopholes and make the statutes generally tougher on hazers. For example, Texas's law was eventually strengthened so that group members who fail to report a hazing may be held accountable, though in 1999 some legal experts said it was unconstitutional.

ESTABLISHING THE BOUNDARIES

Deciding whether an action is a criminal hazing or noncriminal hazing can only be done on a state-by-state basis, depending on the strength of the existing law. One reason that hazing is difficult to regulate nationally at the high school level is that an initiation with potential misdemeanor penalties in one state is a noncriminal offense in another. Some states have laws stipulating that no hazing occurs unless there is bodily injury. Some states say that an initiation qualifies as hazing even if a victim consents to some or all of an initiation, while some states, such as Alabama, look unfavorably on an injured party who willingly participated in many or all initiation practices.

The New York hazing law helped a high school paddling victim press civil charges. John Isaacson successfully sued eight individual members of a fraternity, likely making him the first person to win a judgment in a high school hazing case. The award totaled $150,000. "It clearly shows liability and demonstrates that those who are involved in illegal hazing must bear the brunt of their actions," Isaacson's attorney told a reporter.[2]

In the weeks before Eileen Stevens took the stage in 1999 to receive her honorary degree, she saw evidence that stricter hazing laws were still needed in New York. In April 1999, at Alfred State College, six members of Psi Delta Omega fraternity were charged with various counts of harassment with physical contact and second-degree hazing in an incident that occurred in the group's fraternity house. The school yanked the group's charter immediately.[3]

Nonetheless, Stevens would still like hazing laws to be tougher. An examination of hazing convictions in Missouri, North Carolina, and other states reveals that young people found guilty following initiations rarely spend time in jail. While those who cause the death of another person while drinking and driving can expect sentences of a year or longer in many states, convicted hazers can expect community service or a few weeks or months in jail at most.

Even with antihazing statutes, many local prosecutors seek to press other charges that are easier to prosecute. The prosecutor in Nick Haben's case pursued the harder-to-refute charges of serving alcohol to a minor against the veteran lacrosse players at Western Illinois University. And in 1999, after a simulated sexual assault in a high school athletic hazing left one rookie ballplayer unconscious, an Idaho court convicted an eighteen-year-old defendant on two counts of misdemeanor battery and gave him three months in county jail.[4]

NIKKI'S BATTLE IN MINNESOTA

Nikki Cosentino, a Minnesota teen and professional actress (who has appeared in the movies *Grumpier Old Men* and *Jingle All the Way*), learned about hazing from firsthand experience. As a student at Roseville High School, Nikki was involved in a traditional kidnapping of new sophomores that turned violent as a mob of about 100 students—many intoxicated—overpowered her and several other younger girls and boys. Some urinated on the sophomores, others dyed the victims' hair and broke eggs and bottles on their heads. Nikki subsequently transferred to another high school and, with her mother Mary, lobbied for the passage of an antihazing bill in Minnesota. Nikki's activism angered her former schoolmates and one scratched an obscene word into the paint of Nikki's car. Nonetheless, the Minnesota bill was passed, making it easier for hazing victims to file civil suits against those who hurt them or demean them in hazings.[5]

"No matter what, the pain of coming forward and telling your story is important to save the lives of others," says Nikki Cosentino. "In the long run, your voice will change the unacceptable behavior of your peers and no one deserves to be mistreated!" Nikki's mother, Mary Cosentino, adds, "Always stand up for what you believe in, even if you stand alone! Your voice is the power to make change!"

On occasion, prosecutors have backed off from pressing charges if schools have already taken disciplinary action. The failure of a prosecutor to file charges meets with mixed feelings from the public. On one hand, students without a prior record have an opportunity to shape up without the burden of a permanent criminal record. On the other hand, some activists fear that hazing laws lose clout if they are rarely invoked. Others worry that politics play a part in a prosecutor's reluctance to press charges, particularly if those involved are the children of influential parents or are well known for their athletic participation.

In the state of Washington, the King County prosecutor's office declined to prosecute ten students on hazing charges after Interlake High School expelled the nine students under its jurisdiction. In that 1998 incident, six male and one female eighth grader had to jump into a lake and were coated with food and shaving cream. Interlake High

School principal David Engle said he was unconcerned that charges were not filed since the school's punishment was already severe.[6]

LITIGATION IN COLLEGE AND HIGH SCHOOL HAZING CASES

Perhaps because victims have gotten so little satisfaction in criminal courts, lawsuits against hazers in college—and even high school—have become more common. Many attorneys consider representing hazing victims more seriously than they did in the 1970s, when most would have passed on such cases. A Cincinnati, Ohio, law firm has even published a specialty publication called *Fraternal Law*.

Douglas Fierberg, an attorney in Washington, D.C., has earned a reputation for his expertise in pursuing cases against national fraternities and sororities. When he considers the merits of a case, he asks the following two questions in particular: Was there a history of negligence or bad behavior associated with the organization? After a hazing incident, did the fraternity and/or university take swift, uncompromising action to penalize the individuals and fraternal chapter? If an organization has a history of tolerating hazing incidents and takes no responsibility for preventing future incidents, it is more likely to be found liable.

A few high school cases that have resulted in costly settlements against school districts point out how far many high school districts are behind colleges and Greek-letter groups when it comes to hazing prevention and liability. School districts and parents of hazers risk thousands, perhaps millions of dollars, in real and punitive damages should an unchecked pattern of hazing eventually lead to a death or maiming of an initiate or rookie.

In February 1999, the South Carolina Senate passed a measure requiring the state's department of education to work to end hazing in its public schools. Lawmakers were motivated by a $45,000 judgment in court. The two students sued for being required "to act as prostitutes and assume sexually explicit positions" in a band camp run by the Hedgesville High School band, according to the *Charleston Daily Mail*. The two students were fourteen years old at the time of the hazing.[7]

In January 1995, the state of Washington's Sunnyside school district was slapped with a $5 million lawsuit by a student wrestler who claimed he had been anally penetrated with a mop. The case was settled out of court. While taxpayers customarily have a right to know how much decisions by their public employees are costing them, Sunnyside officials refused to divulge the amount of the settlement. The state's attorney general vowed that future settlements would not be kept from taxpayers.[8]

"In the case of the alleged mop handle rape, [citizens] do not have the results of a criminal trial to tell them whether school officials provided proper protection to the self-professed victim," proclaimed a *Lewiston Morning Tribune* editorial. "The criminal case was thrown out after law enforcement officials bungled handling of the evidence. That left the disposition of the civil suit as the best means of learning whether school officials bear any responsibility for such a disturbing allegation. And now that means has been erased. That is more than a shame. It is a disgrace."

Chances are such a disgrace will be repeated unless attorney generals in other states serve notice that school boards must disclose all details in hazing cases. In 1997, the Poway school district in San Diego, California, paid $675,000 to settle a suit filed by a rookie baseball player penetrated with a broomstick by two veteran teammates. A local newspaper charged the school board with fostering a conspiracy of silence in the case in which details were kept from the public for more than a year. The *San Diego Union-Tribune* wanted the school board to respond to charges that hazing was out of control in the school's athletic program. It also wanted to know what the district had done to prevent future initiations.[9]

Chapter Eight

CAN HAZING BE STOPPED?

If hazing in the United States is to be stopped or even curtailed, it must be attacked as the pervasive social problem that it is. If addressed as a problem in health and social studies classes, hazing can perhaps be best understood in the context of other human rights abuses such as racism and harassment. Hazing is also closely connected to other social issues, such as alcohol abuse, lack of leadership in educational institutions, and risky and abusive behaviors in all segments of the population. Unlike some social evils, this practice can turn deadly.

However, before hazing can be phased out in U.S. colleges and the military, it must first be checked in elementary, middle, and high schools. Just as schools have programs for fire prevention, they should have clearly written policies forbidding hazing—as well as clear provisos for punishment in the event of infractions. The benefits are twofold. First, students who become aware of hazing dangers early on may speak out when they see dangerous initiations in high school. Second, after graduation, they may be more likely to refrain from the practice in college or the military.

HOW TO ATTACK HAZING

The best time for high schools to halt hazing traditions is to attack it preventively—before danger occurs and before battle lines are drawn between administrators, coaches, parents, and students. The challenge for all concerned, therefore, is to learn from the high schools that have endured hazing scandals, eliminated all "wrongs of passage," and established easily understood boundaries about what will and won't be permitted. The issue is as related to good management as it is to safety.

Here are some suggestions to help end hazing.

1. *Help establish welcome programs for first-year and transfer students*

   Rites of passage for teenagers as they grow into young adulthood are valuable and necessary, anthropologists say. Some 200 high schools in the United States have instituted positive, self-esteem-building programs to welcome freshmen. High schools could learn much from the national collegiate fraternities that have established mentor programs as an alternative to the old pledging programs that belittled prospective members. Instead of older students bossing freshmen around, older students can help smooth the way for new students, address fears about their new environment, and offer academic tutoring in a pinch.

   Before good traditions can begin, the old dangerous ones must be outlawed. In 1998, for example, Burrillville High School in Rhode Island scrapped a twenty-year tradition of having first-year students voluntarily humiliate themselves in front of the school's seniors at the annual September Welcome Back Dance. In the past, seniors initiated freshmen by drenching them with water, coating their heads with gel, and painting the letter *F* on their faces.[1]

Burrillville officials decided to get rid of the practice after fielding complaints from parents following the 1997 dance. It was only a matter of time, they decided, before an injury occurred or an offended student brought suit against school officials. Some students disagreed with the new policy, saying all freshman participation was voluntary. Of course, no victim of hazing—pressured by older students—can really be said to give consent.

2. *Reconsider all traditions in all school groups*

Hazing can occur almost anywhere in a high school setting. Sometimes class hazing is strong, with upperclassmen ganging up on sophomores or freshmen. In Arlington, Texas, for example, a high school canceled a long-standing initiation called Howdy Day in which juniors initiate sophomores and seniors initiated both sophomores and juniors. The administration decided that the potential for abuse was too great.

But hazing in athletic teams, the school band, or clubs is often harder to eliminate, particularly if it has the support of a coach or faculty adviser. Such traditions carry on until injury or even arrest occurs. For example, a Concord Township, Ohio, prosecutor looking into paddling allegations against members of a Mentor High School chorus group said that the initiation had taken place in secret for years and included use of a paddling board, which could have caused serious damage to the kidneys.[2]

3. *Don't get caught up in groupthink*

Behavior experts blame groupthink when people in groups fail to intervene to help someone during hazing initiations. Behavior that would be unthinkable under most circumstances is often perceived as acceptable in a group. "So many young people do not have any training in how to be responsible group members," says Rachel Lauer, a social psychology teacher and counselor. "They don't have any way of stopping each other. It's not part of their group rules."[3]

Sociologist Lionel Tiger emphasizes that for teenagers and young college students, loyalty to the group far outweighs moral qualms about the activity. Hence, students who refuse to go along with the crowd need not only approval but support from adults and other teenagers. In addition to educational programs that explain the risks of hazing, students need a crash course about how to refuse to be initiated and to resist initiating others.[4] Older students should try to set a good example by resisting hazing and younger students will likely follow.

4. *Urge your school to adopt a statement of awareness*

   Many schools that have not had serious hazing problems have distributed copies of a hazing policy anyway to students, parents, coaches, and teachers. All who read the policy then sign a statement saying that they will abide by it. Such a statement can go a long way toward making sure ignorance of a hazing statute is no excuse for breaking it. At Leonia High School in New Jersey, student athletes who refuse to sign the policy cannot participate in team sports.[5]

5. *Create a spirit of camaraderie*

   Many high school sports teams and organizations such as the band now create a caste system by having rookies and/or first-year players carry equipment and perform other chores while older players look on or jeer. Coaches, band leaders, and other educators instead can encourage a spirit of cooperation by having all players participate in these chores on a rotation basis.

6. *Urge your school to take precautions to prevent hazing on team buses, in locker rooms, and during trips*

   Coaches cannot be everywhere, but someone in authority can be present in the locker room, on the team bus, and in dormitories at preseason camps to make sure hazing is nonexistent (as well as to enforce all other team regulations). The presence of an adult, especially on school buses, is a strong deterrent. In some states, any coach who allows hazing to go on in his or her presence risks arrest, being hit with a lawsuit, and losing his or her job.

   Precautions are necessary in high-risk situations. When football players leave for training in a remote camp, for example, there must be planned activities for the team's free time and a system in place to send home anyone who initiates or picks on rookie teammates. There should be no question that hazing will be punished if it occurs.

7. *Tell a parent or another responsible adult when you need help. Don't cover up hazing incidents*

   Teammates, class members, teachers, coaches, and administrators often point fingers at one another when hazing occurs, but when rumors of hazing surface in a secondary school, everyone must take responsibility for discussing the unpleasant subject.

   Reporting abuse is not squealing, and it is not wrong. Covering up hazing is always wrong and makes you part of a conspiracy of silence. If a student cannot persuade peers to stop hazing and even school coaches or educators talk about "the need for tradition," it is time to get outside help—fast.

8. *Don't reduce the risk of hazing, eliminate it*

Too often when high school students get caught hazing, they respond with promises to reduce the level of hazing. The problem is too widespread to be fixed by merely toning things down. Hazing is forbidden by many state statutes and against the policies of many schools. You wouldn't say you were cutting down on your stealing if you were caught shoplifting, would you?

Reducing the risk of hazing this year almost guarantees that it will exist in some form next year. It is hardly better than having no plan of action to end hazing at all. Especially when hazing consists of alcohol chugging, sexual assaults, paddling, or beatings, what is demanded is a zero-tolerance attitude, not a tolerant attitude.

9. *Contact hazing activists for guidance and information*

High school students and their parents can be overwhelmed by trying to fight an entire school district alone. Remember, there are hazing activists and groups that can give you guidance when fighting problems in your school. See the For Further Information section at the end of this book for some valuable contacts that can help with sound advice or just keep you up on developments in hazing legislation, hazing reforms, and other hazing news.

10. *If you are involved in a hazing incident, don't be afraid to seek counseling*

Because a number of high school and college students have experienced a post-traumatic stress disorder after enduring hazings, the help of trained counselors can be vital. And because hazers inevitably turn out to have been hazed themselves a year or so earlier, it is also advisable for hazers to seek counseling in order to help break the cycle.

11. *Write to your representatives in state government*

One of the benefits of living in a democracy is that you can voice your opinion. If you live in a state that does not have a hazing law yet, or if your state seems to have a weak one, write a letter to your state representative explaining why you think a hazing law is essential. When activist Eileen Stevens was unable to convince her state senator that a law was needed in New York, she and a friend bought 500 postcards, addressed them to the senator, and asked people to mail them. The message was heard. New York now has one of the stronger antihazing laws.

12. *Get involved in the prevention of gangs*

Until communities organize themselves to keep gang members from recruiting young children and adolescents, the problems and crimes associated with gangs will continue. Some communities have had success when former gang members who have repudiated their old lives return to their neighborhood to share their stories and experience.

The spread of gangs to small towns and suburbs is serving as a wake-up call. Whether because of racism or indifference, too few outsiders tried to help minority communities when gang activity accelerated in the 1960s and 1970s. Far more research into the gang phenomenon is needed. If the economy takes a downturn, the failure to halt the initiation of new gang members may be reflected in more crime, more violence, and growth in the number and size of gangs.

13. *Complain to sports channels and the news media about athletic hazing*

Given the lack of leadership by commissioners in professional football, baseball, and basketball who have failed to step forward to ban hazing initiations, there is little chance that a condemnation of the practice will come from the pros until a top-rated rookie is injured and sues for a lifetime's salary plus damages for pain and mental anguish. Just as revelations by basketball star Magic Johnson put the world on notice in a matter of hours that athletes were not immune to AIDS, so too would the arrest of a superstar football or basketball player accused of hazing speed up the process of eliminating the problem in athletics.

Neither professional sports nor college sports have produced a single public service message about the dangers of hazing. In 1999, however, researchers at Alfred University in New York, in conjunction with the National Collegiate Athletic Association (NCAA), conducted a nationwide survey of NCAA athletes and coaches about attitudes toward hazing. It was the first of its kind and an important step toward spreading awareness among athletes in all sports.

The movement to eliminate athletic hazing would also be furthered if network news programs ran hard-hitting features on initiation practices among amateur and professional athletes. Such investigative reports might result in public indignation and demands for the elimination of hazing at all levels. For too long many sportswriters have looked the other way when hazings occur, or have even condoned such initiations as examples of collegiate humor. For example, in 1999, a *Sports Illustrated* columnist praised hazing in a column that outraged several hazing victims and the parents of a student killed in a hazing incident. The next time you see pro initiations being treated lightly on a sports channel, in a sports magazine, or in your local newspaper, sit down and write a letter.

Unfortunately, many newspaper editorials also reflect the seat-of-the-pants judgments and stereotypical beliefs about hazing that probably go back to the writers' own schooldays. Few know, for example, that the Society of Professional Journalists (SPJ), founded at DePauw University, was very much like a fraternity with Greek letters and secret handshakes. All of the group's early founders belonged to fraternities with their own traditions of hazing. Journalists need to realize that historically many members of the press have taken a very weak stand against hazing.

14. *Don't try at school what you see on television*

Children's television network shows, game shows, and talk shows often have guests talking trash and abusing one another by throwing pies and punches, among other stunts, apparently for fun. Doing these activities in a group situation, even if the initiates claim to be willing participants, is reckless and could quickly accelerate into criminal hazing. Find positive and welcoming ways to bond—period.

15. *Don't confuse discipline with abuse*

Many coaches make their players go to class, learn the fundamentals, think as a team instead of as individuals, and work hard in every practice and game from start to finish. That is discipline. When a coach shoves or taunts a player, that is abuse. Players should accept discipline. They should report abuse to school administrators or a trusted adult immediately.

SOURCE NOTES

CHAPTER ONE

1. "Hazing Kills Schoolboy," *New York Times*, February 11, 1905.
2. Hank Nuwer, "Dead Souls of Hell Week," *Human Behavior*, October 1978, pp. 53–55.
3. Janny Scott, "Group Psychology Explains Police Brutality," in *Police Brutality* (San Diego: Greenhaven Press, 1991), pp. 74–75.
4. Nuwer, "Dead Souls," p. 55.
5. John Berger et al. *Ways of Seeing* (London: BBC and Penguin Books, 1972), pp. 131–133.
6. Hank Nuwer, *Broken Pledges: The Deadly Rite of Hazing* (Atlanta: Longstreet Press, 1990), pp. 203–205.

CHAPTER TWO

1. Anthony Thornton, "McAlester Parents Want Stricter Penalty in Hazing Incident," *Daily Oklahoman*, February 10, 1999.
2. Michael Coit, "Police Drop Wrestler Hazing Probe," (Los Angeles) *Daily News*, January 27, 1998; see also *Los Angeles Times*, September 24, 1997.
3. Pat Wilson, "Writing the Rules on Student Rites," *Pittsburgh Post-Gazette*, January 28, 1998.
4. Christopher Munsey, "Teen 'Paddlers' Charged," (Annapolis, Maryland) *Capital*, July 2, 1998.
5. Robert Tharp, "Another Lamar Student Pleads Guilty in 1996 Hazing Incident," *Fort Worth* (Texas) *Star-Telegram*, October 17, 1997.
6. Carol Chmelynski, National School Board Association News Service online report, *The Education Digest*, Vol. 63, No. 3, 1997.

7. Cheryl Thompson and Ted Gregory, "Pompom Initiation Goes Overboard," *Chicago Tribune*, February 28, 1993.
8. Richard Boyd, "59 Stand Accused in Frat Bash," (New Orleans) *Times-Picayune*, February 24, 1999.
9. Permission to quote from this essay given by Mark Patterson, April 22, 1998.
10. Mike Lindblom and Tamyra Howser, "Hazing Arrests Examples of '90s Concerns," *Seattle Times*, June 18, 1998.
11. Jennifer Van Doren, "Seven Suspended in Sorority Hazing," *Record* (Bergen County, New Jersey), December 21, 1996.
12. *Boston Globe*, December 20, 1992.
13. Wilson, "Writing the Rules on Student Rites."
14. Deerfield police later issued disorderly conduct tickets to eight students. See Brenda Ingersoll, "8 Deerfield Students Ticketed for Hazing," *Wisconsin State Journal*, February 10, 1998.
15. See State of Maryland Case Number CAL86-07253.
16. United Press International, August 8, 1981.
17. Wilson, "Writing the Rules on Student Rites."
18. Cathy Cummins, "Four Boys Beaten by Fellow Students at Overland High," *Rocky Mountain News* (Denver, Colorado), October 15, 1997.

CHAPTER THREE

1. Karen Hucks, "Taking a Closer Look at Bullies," *News Tribune* (Tacoma, Washington), December 19, 1998.
2. Daniel Goleman, "Teen-Age Risktaking," *New York Times*, November 24, 1987.
3. Ibid.
4. Ibid.
5. "40 Day Hazing Probe Ends," *Ventura County* (California) *Star*, February 1, 1998.
6. J. L. Freedman et al, "Compliance without Pressure: The Effect of Guilt," *Journal of Personality and Social Psychology*, 1967, 7, pp. 117–124.

7. R. F. Peck and R. J. Havighurst, *The Psychology of Character Development* (New York: Wiley, 1960), pp. 139–140.
8. Latané Bibb and John M. Darley, "Group Inhibition of Bystanders in Emergencies," *Journal of Personality and Social Psychology,* 1968, 9, pp. 142–146.
9. Erik H. Erikson, *Identity: Youth and Crisis* (New York: Norton, 1968), p. 87.
10. *Detroit News,* November 5, 1995.
11. Greg Toppo, "'Kidnappings' During Homecoming Not New," *Santa Fe New Mexican,* October 24, 1997.
12. I would like to thank Jon and Lynn Franklin for making me aware of this quotation from Charles Dickens.
13. *The Bulletin* (Bend, Oregon), October 18, 1996.
14. Victor Raskin, "Psychological Theories of Humor," *Psychology Today,* volume 19, number 10, p. 39.
15. Mike Lindblom and Tamyra Howser, "Interlake High School Students Arrested This Week," *Seattle Times,* June 18, 1998.
16. Edgar Z. Friedenberg, *Coming of Age in America: Growth and Acquiescence* (New York: Vintage, 1965), p. 218.
17. Ibid, pp. 219–220. I am grateful to Elizabeth Barrett for suggesting additional reading materials in the area of harassment of gay and lesbian high school students.
18. Ibid, p. 222.

CHAPTER FOUR
1. United Press International, May 8, 1992.
2. Lisa Cripe, "Hazing: Rite of Passage?" *Spokane* (Washington) *Spokesman-Review,* October 19, 1998.
3. United Press International, December 3, 1981.
4. United Press International, September 14 and October 2, 1984.
5. "Johnson Creek Wrestlers Cleared of Charges," United Press International, September 26, 1992.
6. Nicholas K. Geranios, "Small Town Grapples with Wrestler's Alleged Rape," *Allentown* (Pennsylvania) *Morning Call,* February 24, 1992.

7. Jim MacLaughlin, "High School 'Hazings' Ignite Parent Concerns," *Boston Globe*, November 18, 1985.

8. Kathy Scrizzi, "Board Bars Five LHS Players from Team," *Boston Globe*, November 21, 1985.

9. Peter S. Canellos, "Grid Camp Hazing Shocks Watertown," *Boston Globe*, October 15, 1988.

10. Susan Hershey, "Lenaghan Is Disappointed with Attitude Toward Hazing," *Watertown* (Massachusetts) *Sun*, October 12, 1988.

11. John Vellante, "Time for Healing to Begin in Wilmington," *Boston Globe*, October 25, 1992.

12. Nuwer, *Broken Pledges*, p. 50.

13. Leslie Weaver, "High School Hazing Still Uncharted Area," *Record* (Bergen County, New Jersey), November 12, 1989.

14. Sherry Figdore, "Parents, Teens Protest Hazing Charges," *Asbury Park Press* (Neptune, New York), November 7, 1997.

15. Nuwer, *Broken Pledges*, pp. 57–58.

16. Peg McEntee, "Hazing Victim's Last Claim Dismissed," *Salt Lake Tribune*, September 12, 1998. I also appeared on *ABC Home Show* in Los Angeles and discussed the case with the victim's parents.

17. Richard Cowen, "Athletes Agree to Refrain," *Record* (Bergen County, New Jersey), December 4, 1998.

18. Ellen Miller, "Meeker Families to Sue Coach," *Denver Post*, March 15, 1997.

19. *Rocky Mountain News* (Denver, Colorado), November 26, 1998.

20. Phil Boas, "Grid Glory Desire to Win Clouds Judgment on New Gilbert Coach," (Phoenix) *Arizona Republic*, March 10, 1999.

21. Ibid.

22. Craig Morgan, Melissa Jones, and Richard Obert, "Busken Accused of Directing Hazing," *Arizona Republic*, November 13, 1998.

23. Letters to the Editor, *Arizona Republic*, December 4, 1998.

24. Shelby Oppel, "Board Criticizes Discipline in Hazing," *North Pinellas* (Florida) *Times*, March 11, 1998.
25. Steve Warmbir, "Brothers Describe Assault of Prep Football Player," *Chicago Daily Herald*, March 10, 1999.
26. Cox News Service article, September 22, 1998.

CHAPTER FIVE

1. Lynn Okamoto, "Reports Point to a Rise in Hazing across Country," *Des Moines Register*, September 6, 1998.
2. Ibid.
3. Jeannie Johnson and S. U. Mahesh, "Hazing Results in Santa Fe Suspensions," *Albuquerque Journal*, October 25, 1997.
4. "Fraternity Members Face Drinking Charges," *Advocate* (Baton Rouge, Louisiana), February 22, 1999; Ed Anderson, "LSU Frat Fined in Pledge's Death," *Times-Picayune*, September 1, 1998.
5. Goleman, "Teen-Age Risktaking."
6. Oxtoby was never accused of any crime by police or sued by the Habens in civil court. Western Illinois University did not imply wrongdoing or legal responsibility on Oxtoby's part. Oxtoby remained at Western Illinois University as a librarian and has received awards and recognitions for his outstanding work with fraternity members. He no longer coaches sports clubs at the university, however.
7. Jason Altenbern, "Letter to the Editor: Person Hazed Was Scared, Not Naive," *Western* (Illinois University) *Courier*, September 17, 1993.
8. Nick Haben's wallet was lost along the river, was found by two students, and was returned to the Habens through the school.
9. Alice Haben received notes of condolence from WIU President Ralph H. Wagoner and Ronald D. Gierhan, vice president for student services, October 24, 1990.

10. Editorial, *Western* (Illinois University) *Courier*, September 15, 1993.
11. "Students Charged in Hazing Incident Plead Not Guilty," (Springfield, Illinois) *State Journal-Register*, October 9, 1998.
12. Dave Walker, "Role May Be a Great Catch for Bonds," *Arizona Republic*, April 11, 1994.

CHAPTER SIX

1. Joan Moore, "Gangs, Drugs, and Violence," in *Gangs*, edited by Scott Cummings and Daniel J. Monti (Albany: State University of New York Press, 1993), pp. 27–32.
2. Will Higgins, "Gangs Stake Claim to Main Street," *Indianapolis Star*, October 26, 1995.
3. S. K. Bardwell, " 'Animal-like' Gang Initiation Snared 2 Girls," *Houston Chronicle*, July 1, 1993.
4. United Press International, July 5, 1989.
5. Lynne K. Varner, "Youth Pleads Guilty in Boy's Death, *Seattle Post-Intelligencer*, September 15, 1994.
6. Rosalind Miles, *Love, Sex, Death and the Making of the Male* (New York: Summit Books, 1991), p. 89.
7. Ibid.
8. David J. Bordua, "Delinquent Subcultures: Sociological Interpretations of Gang Delinquency," in *Annals of the American Academy of Political and Social Science*, November 1961, Reprint Edition, p. 123 and p. 126.
9. Miles, p. 93.
10. Bordua, "Delinquent Subcultures," pp. 120–121.
11. Rick Landre, Mike Miller, Dee Porter, *Gangs: A Handbook for Community Awareness* (New York: Facts on File, Inc., 1997), p. 134.
12. Richard W. Jaeger, "Youth Gangs Emerging in Wisconsin's Small Towns," *Wisconsin State Journal*, May 25, 1997.
13. *Orlando Sentinel*, October 24, 1996.
14. *Washington Post*, September 14, 1996.

15. Richard W. Jaeger, "Youth Gangs Emerging in Wisconsin's Small Towns," *Wisconsin State Journal*, May 25, 1997.
16. Landre, Miller, Porter, *Gangs*, pp. 135–137.

CHAPTER SEVEN

1. Goleman, "Teen-Age Risktaking."
2. United Press International, May 16, 1985.
3. "Fraternity Hazing Charged," *Buffalo News*, April 10, 1999.
4. Tara King, "Moliga Gets 3 Months for Bus Incident," *Lewiston Morning Tribune*, April 9, 1999.
5. Rob Hotakainen and Gregor W. Phinney, "Mom, Teen Lead Push for Anti-Hazing Bill," *Minneapolis Star Tribune*, January 17, 1997.
6. "No Charges in Hazing," *Seattle Times*, September 3, 1998.
7. "Bill Addressing Hazing in Schools," *Charleston Daily Mail*, February 25, 1999.
8. Editorial, *Lewiston Morning Tribune*, January 5, 1995.
9. "Nagging Doubts; Rape Settlement Swathed in Secrecy," *San Diego Union-Tribune*, August 5, 1998.

CHAPTER EIGHT

1. Drake Witham, "Annual Freshman Welcome Is Getting a Little Tamer This Year," *Providence* (Rhode Island) *Journal-Bulletin*, September 18, 1998.
2. "9 Chorus Members Charged in Hazing Ritual at School," *Columbus Dispatch,* September 20, 1996.
3. Weaver, "High School Hazing."
4. Goleman, "Teen-Age Risktaking."
5. Cowen, "Athletes Agree to Refrain."

FOR FURTHER INFORMATION

BOOKS

Akers, Ronald L. *Deviant Behavior: A Social Learning Approach*. Belmont, Calif.: Wadsworth, 1985.

Arnold, James, and George D. Kuh. *Brotherhood and the Bottle: A Cultural Analysis of the Role of Alcohol in Fraternities*. Bloomington, Ind.: Center for the Study of the Fraternity, 1992.

Kaplan, Leslie. *Coping with Peer Pressure*. Center City, Minn.: Hazelden Information Education, 1997.

Landre, Rick, Mike Miller, and Dee Porter. *Gangs: A Handbook for Community Awareness*. New York: Facts on File, 1997.

Miedzian, Myriam. *Boys Will Be Boys: Breaking the Link between Masculinity and Violence*. New York: Doubleday, 1992.

Miles, Rosalind. *Love, Sex, Death, and the Making of the Male*. New York: Summit Books, 1991.

Nuwer, Hank. *Broken Pledges: The Deadly Rite of Hazing*. Atlanta, Ga.: Longstreet, 1990.

Nuwer, Hank. *Wrongs of Passage: Fraternities, Sororities, Hazing and Binge Drinking*. Bloomington: Indiana University Press, 1999.

Rodriquez, Joseph, et al. *East Side Stories: Gang Life in East L.A.* New York: Power House Cultural Entertainment, 1998.

Sikes, Gini. *8 Ball Chicks: A Year in the Violent World of Girl Gangsters*. New York: Anchor Books, 1997.

WEB SITES

StopHazing.org
http://stophazing.org/
> Founded in 1993 at the University of New Hampshire, the StopHazing group has expanded to Vermont, Georgia, Massachusetts, and Ohio and supports antihazing efforts across the nation. This web site provides links to new hazing sites.

Security on Campus, Inc. (SOC)
http://campussafety.org/
> The only national nonprofit organization geared exclusively to the prevention of college and university campus violence and other crimes such as hazing. This web site offers information and links about relevant laws and other assistance organizations.

Alfred University
http://www.alfred.edu/
> This web site offers information about the 1999 national survey of college athletic hazing practices conducted by the university and the National Collegiate Athletic Association.

GreekNet
http://www.greeknet.net
> This web site provides links to fraternal groups working to end hazing.

Wrongs of Passage
http://sites.netscape.net/hanknuwer/homepage
> This web site, maintained by the author, provides updates on hazing legislation and news.

ANTIHAZING ORGANIZATIONS AND ACTIVISTS

The Committee to Halt Useless College Killings (CHUCK)
c/o Eileen Stevens
P.O. Box 188
Sayville, NY 11782

Cease Hazing Activities and Deaths (CHAD)
c/o Rita Saucier
P.O. Box 850955
Mobile, AL 36685

Alice Haben
P.O. Box 143
Oswego, IL 60543

Anti-Hazing Initiatives
c/o Nikki Cosentino and Mary Cosentino
P.O. Box 136
1769 Lexington Avenue
Roseville, MN 55113
http://www.anti-hazing.qpg.com/

Security on Campus, Inc. (SOC)
c/o Connie Clery
215 West Church Road, Suite 200
King of Prussia, PA 19406

The National Fraternity Conference (NIC)
3901 West 86th Street, Suite 390
Indianapolis, IN 46268
> The NIC sells videos on hazing and runs Adopt-a-School, a program in which college students form relationships with elementary schoolchildren.

INDEX

Page numbers in *italics* indicate illustrations.

ABOUT THE AUTHOR

Hank Nuwer has written about hazing for more than twenty years. Known internationally for his publications on hazing and his hazing news service for educators and journalists, he has spoken at Cornell University, Indiana University, and the University of Colorado, among others.

Nuwer is the author of two other books on hazing, *Wrongs of Passage* (Indiana University Press) and *Broken Pledges: The Deadly Rite of Hazing*, articles for the *New York Times Sunday Magazine*, *Human Behavior*, and *Harper's Magazine*, and several books for Franklin Watts, most recently *The Legend of Jesse Owens*. He also worked as a consultant on the television movie *Moment of Truth: Broken Pledges*.

Hank Nuwer has taught journalism since 1982 and is currently an adjunct professor at Indiana University-Purdue University and Anderson University. He was named a 1999 outstanding alumnus of Buffalo State College in New York.